HEIRS TOGETHER
OF LIFE

I thank God for
our friendship.
                    Dottie Piper

November 1982

HEIRS TOGETHER
OF LIFE

Charles H. and Norma R. Ellis

THE BANNER OF TRUTH TRUST

THE BANNER OF TRUTH TRUST
3 Murrayfield Road, Edinburgh EH12 6EL
P O Box 621, Carlisle, Pennsylvania 17013, U.S.A.

✳

© *Charles & Norma Ellis* 1980
First published 1980
ISBN 0 85151 311 5

✳

Printed and bound in the U.S.A. by Fairfield Graphics

To
Raymond, Dorothy, Carol,
Elaine, Virginia,
Richard and John
(who know where we have failed,
but know, too, how gracious God has been
to our family)

Contents

[viii]

[xii]

Preface

'Likewise, ye husbands, dwell with them according to knowledge, giving honor unto the wife, as unto the weaker vessel, and as being heirs together of the grace of life; that your prayers be not hindered' (1 Peter 3:7).

When our Saviour died, He named us in His will! He made provision that as man and wife we should receive life-abundant, three-dimensional life which is eternal. As recipients of this legacy we are not just to sit down and bask in our gift. We are to allow this gift to have an effect upon us. We are to live this life now. As heirs together we are to live in a loving, considerate unity, not allowing discord or lack of esteem and respect to mar our relationship and hinder our fellowship together with our Lord. Truly, God has given us eternal life, but we are to work out our own salvation, knowing at the same time that it is He who is working in us (Philippians 2:12–13).

We have here prepared a study of God's Word, beginning 'in the beginning' and going through to the eternal kingdom, to discover what He has revealed concerning His will and provision for men and women and their relationship with one another. We hope this study will assist many in understanding more thoroughly what the

Creator has designed for marriage and the home.

Since the basis for this guide is God's Word, we believe it would have value for any reader. But it is especially prepared for couples. We urge that, in accordance with God's plan, the husband lead his wife in a daily devotional period. First the designated Scripture and the commentary should be read. The Authorized Version is used here, since probably the majority of Christians have this available. The comments are generally based upon this version, although some quotations are from the New American Standard Bible (NASB) or the New International Version (NIV) when they are considered to be more clear or closer to the original. The Scripture reading is the most important part of this devotional exercise. The comments are not meant to stand alone, but to open up the Scripture and apply it specifically to the home.

After the reading, time should be given for the sharing of reactions and opinions. It is one thing to read the Bible, but what are you going to do about it? Do the concepts in the Scripture reading flood you with thanksgiving? Then give thanks! Does the reading throw light upon an area in your marriage which needs to be brought into closer conformity with God's revealed will? Then brush away old concepts, clear up misunderstandings and confess sins which have been hindering you from being a unity. Talk together openly, 'speaking the truth in love'! (Ephesians 4:15a). And forgive, even as God has forgiven you!

The time together should be closed with prayer, each partner in turn offering thanks to God for the blessings of the day and presenting before Him the special needs of the home. If praying aloud together is new in your marriage this may be difficult at first, but each day it will grow easier, and you will marvel at the way in which God will answer your prayers and mold you into the kind of relationship He has in mind for you.

It is our hope that by the time you have finished this summary overview you will be so thoroughly patterned that you will continue together in a daily devotional reading for yourselves, digging more deeply into the Scriptures than has been possible here.

'Let the peace of Christ rule in your hearts, since as members of one body you were called to peace. And be thankful' (Col. 3:15 NIV).

Charles and Norma Ellis
Owl's Head, Maine, U.S.A.

GOD MAKES A GOOD WORLD
Genesis 1:1–25

All that *is* is from the mind, the power, the hand of God the Creator. God made each thing to be a certain way, perfect in itself, fulfilling His purpose for it. As it came from His hand it was 'very good.'

Part of the goodness of the world lies in the fact that each animate thing was equipped to reproduce other individuals like itself, 'after its kind.' The creation was and is self-perpetuating. In myriad ways new members are daily brought into being. The process of male and female cells uniting to form young varies with fern and holly and sea horse and man. But the pattern is the same; parents bring forth new individuals like themselves.

This first chapter of Genesis rules out the possibility of a haphazard, chance-formed universe, gradually evolving, again by chance. It rules out the notion that impersonal matter, plus time, plus chance, results in all that now exists, as Francis Schaeffer expresses it.

It is absolutely basic that we in our homes have an adequate concept of the personal God who had a plan in creation, a plan which extends down through history and through eternity and which embraces us! According to His plan human beings live in families with a father and mother and children. The God-ordained unit of society is the home.

Thank you, heavenly Father, for this good and beautiful world. And thank You for making provision in Your plan for our becoming members of Your special family through Your Son.

GOD MAKES MAN AND WOMAN
Genesis 1:26–31

As the climax and crown of creation, God created the man and the woman. They were an integral part of the earth, being formed from its dust. And along with members of the plant and animal kingdoms they were commanded to reproduce after their kind.

But the man and the woman were made different from the rest of creation. They were created in the image of God! What does this mean? Does this degrade God, suggesting that He is a *Bigger Man?* Impossible! Jesus tells us that God is a Spirit (John 4:24). In no way does this concept degrade God. What it does, rather, is to elevate man. It makes him special, distinct and different from the rest of creation. He was made in the image of God, with dominion over the creatures.

As we grow in our understanding of the implications of this teaching we grow in our respect for God the Creator. But we also grow in our respect for ourselves, for each other, and for our children. We were made in the divine image 'in

[20]

knowledge, righteousness and holiness, with dominion over the creatures'!* We reflect God Himself!

God's children cannot call any man 'trash' (to quote Schaeffer again). We have to see all men, even our children in their recalcitrant moods, as being *wonderful!* God enables us to see in ourselves and others what the unregenerate man cannot see. We can appreciate the nobility that clings to the least attractive of men. After all they are *men,* and men have been granted to share in some of the attributes of the Creator.

Surely this teaching clothes our family with a very special dignity.

GOD MAKES A HOME
Genesis 2:1–17

Following a custom in Hebrew writing, Moses in chapter 2 beginning at verse 4 goes into more detail concerning the matter he had covered previously in broader terms. In the first chapter he had written about the creation of all things, including the man and the woman. Now he focuses our attention specifically on the making of the man and then the woman individually.

Man belongs to the earth, being made from it. He is at home there, equipped physically to inhabit it. But God honored man by stooping

* *Westminster Shorter Catechism,* Question 10

to breathe life into him and man became a living soul. By the divine inbreathing God made him animate creation and specifically man at the same time. This was not a crude being somehow elevated to manhood. At his creation man was made at once what God wanted him to be.

In today's reading it is man's closeness to the earth that is pictured in a significant way. God, the first gardener, made Eden, the first garden, as a home for man. He placed man in it and bade him tend and keep it. What a pleasant and rewarding task Adam was given! He did not have to fight either drought or flood: a rising mist watered the ground. Nor did he have to combat plant or animal pests. The garden yielded luscious fruit. God was good to the man He had made.

At this point in history we as God's children should never lose sight of this picture of the wonderful world that God made and of the way in which He made us to have our home in it, supplied with all we need to sustain us and to satisfy us as persons made in His image. He was pleased to make us beings who needed to have our roots down. He provided us with pleasures derived from having a place that is especially ours on the face of the earth. He made a place for man that was a counterpart to heaven.

Man is not purely spirit, as God is. He is also body. He is bound to the earth until God releases him. So God made him able to enjoy and appreciate the earth and to have a real function in its care, finding fulfilment in his task. We are only sojourners here, but while we are here God wants us to enjoy to the full the home He made for us.

GOD MAKES A COVENANT WITH MAN
Genesis 2:8–17

When God placed man in the garden He was concerned not only with his physical needs but with his whole being. God planned for man the freedom to live a full and complete life. This freedom would be possible only through man's voluntary submission to his Maker and to the pattern of living He had designed for him.

To achieve this end God set aside a certain tree and used it for a test. If man chose the road of obedience to God and resisted the temptation to eat of that tree he would continue to live in freedom under God's plan. If he disobeyed God and ate of the tree, he would die.

The tree had a name, 'the tree of knowledge of good and evil' (2:9). If man obeyed God he would be confirmed in righteousness and so understand that it was good to obey God and evil to disobey Him. If he disobeyed and ate of the tree he would know experientially what sin was and would reap its consequences.

The man understood God's arrangement. As we look back upon it we can call it one of two names. We can call it the covenant of life in that life was the fruit of continuing obedience. Or we can call it the covenant of works since in it

God required a specific act or work of obedience on the part of man in order that he might maintain a right relationship with his Maker.

In 1 Corinthians 15:22 Paul tells us that we were involved in this transaction God made with man. We were there in the garden with Adam, our representative, and what he would do with that tree had a significance beyond the garden. This story of Eden is not academic. What occurred there has had an effect on every man and woman born into this world. To understand this is the first step toward understanding how Jesus Christ the second Adam could have paid the penalty for our sin!

GOD MAKES WOMAN
Genesis 2:18–25

In this beautiful world, fresh from the hand of God, there was man and there were the animals. God brought the animals before man. With a keen insight Adam observed each kind of creature and gave it an appropriate name. These, God said, are your dominion. Look at them. They are yours to be used and enjoyed as a good steward for Me. And each one had a mate.

Did this experience contribute to Adam's sense of aloneness in the world? The animals were perfect as they came from the hand of the Creator. But they had no soul. They were not made in the image of God. Man could not communicate with them the deep warm personal thoughts and emotions within him. He could not say to the horse, 'Would you like to watch the sunset down by the river?' and expect to receive an answer, 'I'd love to!'

John Milton commented, 'Loneliness is the first thing which God's eye nam'd not good.'* God made man to be a social being. And the heavenly Father, demonstrating His love and understanding, proceeded with His plan for creation and made woman to meet his need.

Loneliness *is* bad. God has said this and we can affirm it from our own experience. Yet, because it is bad we shun it and we reach out from ourselves and our isolation to other people, to one person in particular and to God Himself! Man was not made a complete, independent, self-satisfied being. Aloneness or complete independence was not normal or good for him. So God made woman!

Into Adam's aloneness God placed a creature appropriate for him, one exactly right for him. The man and the woman together would form a family unit—a permanent unit, exclusive and beautiful according to God's design!

REBELLION IN THE GARDEN
Genesis 3:1–6

So far our story sounds idyllic. It sounds as though Genesis is out of touch with reality. No wonder, we might say, the Bible is not accepted by many

* *Tetrachordon*

as relevant to our day. This is a myth of Paradise with which we cannot identify.

But wait and see what happened next. The man and woman, with everything in their favor, chose to trust in their own intelligence and indulge their own desires, believing the lie of Satan instead of the truth of God.

They had, in possessing the image of God, the power of choice. As it has been said, there was no electric fence around the tree of the knowledge of good and evil. They were not shut off from it. But neither did they *have* to eat of it. They actively chose to disobey God. They were moral agents. They knew that to obey God was good and to disobey was bad. Adam and Eve, with everything in their favor, with full knowledge of their own responsibility and their power of choice, ate the fruit.

The picture has changed. Sin has moved into the garden like a dark, chilling mist. Now we understand! We see our world taking shape before our eyes—a good, beautiful, tremendous world, but one now soiled, ravaged, polluted, twisted!

Christianity provides the only reasonable explanation for the goodness and badness of life, the nobility and degradation of man, the beauty and ugliness of experience. It is all here in Eden: the pristine holiness and the brilliance of the universe and of life as God created them, but also the sinfulness, the ignorance and the impotence. In Eden we understand reality. The Bible is relevant to life in any age.

[26]

Thank You, God, for giving us the Written Word which explains the things about good and evil that we could learn nowhere else!

ALIENATION IN EDEN
Genesis 3:7–10

When Adam and Eve ate the fruit they did not become poisoned as if the fruit had been contaminated. Their very eating of the fruit, rather, was an indication of a growing spirit of revolt against God. It was the forthright act that gave evidence of rebellion.

Now that they had disobeyed God it was as though a wall were built or as though war had been declared. There was separation, enmity. They were alienated from God. No longer did they have sweet communion with Him as they walked together in the cool of the evening. Now they fled from His presence. There was fear. And 'fear hath torment' (I John 4:18).

Now their own unity was broken, too. They had been made to cleave to each other and be one flesh. But now that sin had defaced the image of God in them they were ashamed. Vainly they attempted to hide from each other behind clothing of leaves. And vainly they attempted to keep from each other the growing ugliness of their thoughts and feelings!

We learn in geometry that if two lines are each parallel to a third line they are parallel to each other. We might say that the third line is the norm and so is like God. If the man is in the right relationship with God and if the woman is in the right relationship with God, then each is in the right relationship with the other. If one of them is askew, then their marriage is distorted.

Has a problem developed in our marriage in any area? Then let us each attempt to discover what is wrong with his/her own relationship with God. If each of us will strive to live in loving submission to God, obeying His principles for marriage, a change will occur. The alienation of Eden cannot persist in the Christian home if both man and woman are seeking to glorify God.

THE FIRST MARRIAGE DISRUPTED
Genesis 3:11–14

We have seen that the first marriage, which in the beginning was a perfect one, was marred because of sin. God planned a relationship in which two persons would experience a beautiful unity with each other and with their Creator. This relationship was disrupted.

Further evidence of this disruption is seen in the way in which Adam blames Eve for his sin. In God's economy the man was made head of the family. The woman was given to help him. Eve should not have been persuaded by Satan to take the fruit. She should not have offered it to Adam. But, even then, Adam did not need to follow her lead. So he had to bear his own guilt before God. The roles as set forth by God were reversed. Responsibility was shed, and ugliness resulted.

Still another evidence of the disruption of the relationship between man and God is seen here. Adam blames God: 'The woman whom *Thou* gavest to be with me . . .' (3:12). And Eve? She claims that Satan beguiled her (3:13). She, too, refuses to shoulder her own blame.

How well we can see ourselves in Adam and Eve! Now we are really beginning to identify with the first couple. Our generation, like theirs, is perennially guilty of failing to act responsibly. How freely we place the blame for our actions on mate, parents, society, God!

Father, make us aware of this failure even in our own marriage which You are redeeming. Help us to say, 'I did it. It was my fault. I'm sorry. Forgive me.' We want our marriage to be the beautiful unity You designed it to be.

GOD'S GRACE IN THE MIDST OF JUDGMENT
Genesis 3:15–21

God had said that Adam and Eve would die if they ate the fruit. They did not at that moment cease from their physical existence. What did God mean?

Along with the rest of creation, the bodies of

Adam and Eve would now be feeling the encroachment of death. They would be experiencing the frailties of the flesh, the disease and weakness that would finally overtake them. This is one of the things that God meant.

But God also meant that they would die spiritually. No longer would they have the same quality of life that had enabled them to have fellowship with God. No longer would they have the deepest fellowship with each other. Now the woman would be, not a helper, but a self-asserting subject, or, at best, something less than a gentle, co-operative follower. In his sin the husband would not, at best, be a completely benign leader. He might be a despot. Or, on the other hand, he might be spineless, abdicating his responsibility. Life as God had designed it would be out of the reach of man.

No longer, either, would the man have the simple task of caring for a fully responsive garden. His task as family head would be complicated by a ground cursed with thorns and thistles. And the woman's joy in bringing forth children would be dulled as her conceptions would be multiplied and the process of birth would be accompanied by pain and distress.

How good of God, in the midst of this blow to the first man and woman, to promise relief! Genesis 3:15 is the first announcement of deliverance in the form of a Saviour. Even here, when God had every right to send immediate destruction because of man's disobedience, He manifested His grace. Now the thread of Messianic prophecy, a thread red as the Saviour's blood, is fastened into the tapestry of written revelation. And we can follow it through to the last page of Scripture. What a gracious God is ours!

ADAM KNEW EVE
Genesis 4:1,25,26

The Hebrew word for *know,* as well as the Greek, has a richness we need to appreciate for our understanding of the Bible. It does not mean mere recognition, 'I knew him a block away.' It does not mean simply insight into a person's character, 'I know her like a book.' It means also *love.* God knew His people. He recognized all of His people. He had the deepest insight into their character and heart. But further, He *loved* them.

And this same word is used here and often in Scripture for the marriage act. Adam knew Eve. Adam loved Eve and God had provided a special means by which he might express his love, a special act of closeness and exclusiveness.

Sex, as God ordained it, is an expression of love, a tangible, special way for the oneness of man and wife to be manifested. God had all of this in mind when He made them male and female in the beginning.

Even after the coming of sin into the world, with the train of distortion and sorrow and tragedy that followed, God has graciously permitted men, even unbelieving men, a suggestion of the joy that is possible in marital love and the family. Marriage is a blessing to all men. What a loss to mankind to minimize the worth of marriage and the family!

But just as God redeems individuals, He redeems marriage. He makes the man and woman new creatures in Christ. And just as the roles of man and woman are reoriented when Christ comes into lives, so is the sex relationship. The Christian man and woman can really *know* each other in the many facets of that rich word 'know'!

THE FIRST FAMILY KNOWS TRAGEDY
Genesis 3:22—4:8

Adam had disobeyed God and the verdict was death. While still in the flesh he was in a state of spiritual death, at enmity with God. What if now he should eat of the tree of life and continue in spiritual death forever? Was it not an act of God's mercy that man was driven from the reach of the fruit of this tree?

But here he was, cast out from the only home he had ever known, estranged from God and also estranged from Eve because of sin. Into such a family situation two boys were born. The joy attending the birth of the first babies into the world was dulled by sin, too. They were born with a sinful nature which they had inherited from their parents. Their environment also was marred by sin. All was not well in the first family.

[32]

However, Adam and Eve had not completely turned from God. Since Genesis 3:15 was the first announcement of the gospel, we may say that in a sense the church had its beginning in Eden. From verse 4 of chapter 4 we know that Abel had absorbed from his home training the facts concerning how to come before God acceptably by means of a blood sacrifice offered in faith. And God received his sacrifice so offered.

But Cain, in jealousy and anger and guilt, could not stand to see his brother enjoying a favor with God which he could not share. He 'rose up against Abel his brother, and slew him' (4:8). Rivalry among brothers and sisters is as old as the family itself!

To this day all homes, unbelieving or Christian, are touched by some sin and tragedy. There is potential for much beauty and joy in the home as God designed it. But only as each member submits to God will the home be what it should and can be—a reflection and foretaste of heaven.

THE BEGINNING OF PRAYER
Genesis 4:25,26

Adam and Eve had talked with God in the garden. But after the fall their communion with Him was broken. They still had conversation with Him, but this was the mere saying of words. They could not speak His language. There was a gulf between them, the gulf between sin and holiness. There was no real communion.

In the providence of God men now learned that they could talk to God in a new way through prayer. Even if the presence of God was not manifested as it had been in Eden they could address Him. They must have been taught by His Holy Spirit that they could speak to their Maker and He would bend low His ear and hear. True, only through Christ may men have access to God. But in the garden men were given a first promise of His coming. And the sacrificial system was a mute testimony to men's need to approach God through the Lamb that He would provide. Even at the dawn of history there must have been communicated to man in a faint way God's plan of salvation. And in the light of the certainty in God's appointed time of the death of His Son to cleanse men from their sin, there was even then the possibility of communion between fallen, sinful men and the holy God.

We, on this side of Calvary, strain to comprehend this account of the inception of prayer. We are used to prayer. It is so common and available! We are not sensitive to what it cost the Father to provide a means by which this communion could be re-established. Do we thank God enough for bridging the gap between us and Himself? Do we really value the gift of prayer?

MIXED MARRIAGES
Genesis 6:1–8

People today, even Christians, sometimes fail to recognize the great cleavage among men. God's Word breaks down national, racial, social, and economic barriers. No one can find in Scripture justification for prohibiting marriage across these lines. But the Bible teaches a great cleavage between the 'daughters of men' and the 'sons of God' which does preclude marriage.

Who were these 'daughters of men'? The indications are that the 'daughters of men' were in the line of Cain, that branch of the family of Adam which had turned from God and made no pretense of being His people.

The 'sons of God,' who would be the line of Seth, had no business marrying these girls. The context makes it quite clear that at this early date men knew the will of God for marriage within the faith.

But why this wording? Why does it not read, 'Some of the sons of God married some of the daughters of men and some of the daughters of God married some of the sons of men.'? Since this is a problem that troubles a number of people, let us make two observations concerning it. First, simply, it would be very awkward sentence structure! Often the reverse of a statement is implied without being stated in order to avoid such clumsiness of style. But second, at this time in history the male was the initiator of marriage plans. He went out to seek a bride. His would be the sin in that he, knowing the will of God, nevertheless actually left his own people and went to seek a bride from outside the faith. One needs to go no further than this to get an understanding of this passage. What God is doing is commenting on the fact that there was disobedience with reference to the choice of a marriage partner.

Jesus said, 'For as in the days that were before the flood they were eating and drinking, marrying and giving in marriage, until the day that Noe entered into the ark . . . so shall also the coming of the Son of man be' (Matthew 24:38,39). How contemporary that sounds! And as then, so now, God's people are guilty of defying His declared will that they are to marry only within the faith. In the sight of God this is the sin of the mixed marriage. Whether we eat or drink or marry, all is to be done to His glory.

THE ARK OF SAFETY
Genesis 6:9–22

As God looked upon the increasing wickedness of men He saw Noah, who 'found grace' in his eyes. 'Noah was a just man and perfect in his generations, and Noah walked with God' (6:9). Noah was righteous not in that he was able of himself to obey God, but in that he believed God and was thus enabled to obey Him.

When God set out to wipe the ungodly from

the earth and make a fresh start, He told Noah
He would make a covenant with Him and with
his wife and his sons and their wives. God would
keep Noah and his family safe in the midst of
the cataclysmic flood.

With all the searching that has been undertaken
will the real ark ever be found? Hundreds of
pages have been written on the search for this
ship. A film has been produced about the search.
Churches have been built according to the specifi-
cations given in Genesis. Toys are available that
are models of the ark—complete with animals
and the family of Noah! The ark is a fascinating
story to adults and children alike.

But this is not simply an interesting tale. It is
also sober history. Christ refers to it as such. And
it is, in a sense, prophecy. It foreshadows the
salvation from just judgment for sin through a
greater than Noah, the Lord Jesus. He is our
ark of safety. In Him men and women today with
their families may find refuge.

GOD'S BOW IN THE SKY
Genesis 9:8–17

God made man with a remarkable power to respond to visual imagery. And He, the First
Teacher, used this characteristic of man as an opportunity for teaching His truth. God employed
visual aids.

In figures of speech—simile, metaphor, allegory, parable—God took things in the visible

world, in the experience of man, and used them to illustrate spiritual truths. The very fact that He made man in His own image was a way of teaching the creature something about the nature of the Creator. As the years went by He used many other things to make clear to our sin-darkened intellects the great and wonderful things of the Spirit. He used marriage, the sheep and the shepherd, the potter and the clay, the vine. He used the Passover, the tabernacle and the whole sacrificial system to teach man of His redemption through the Christ.

And here we read of the rainbow. God set a bow in the sky, a bow fashioned of light and color, faint, fragile, exquisite, real. The rainbow—drops of water transformed by the rays of God's sun—was placed in the sky to remind man of the promise of the Sovereign God never again to destroy mankind by water! Only our God could have thought of that!

What kind of students are we in God's school? Are we learning His truths so aptly taught? And are we wise enough to emulate His methods and His figures as we teach our own children about our Heavenly Father? Do they know about the rainbow? About the Lamb without blemish?

THE FATHER OF THE FAITHFUL
Genesis 12:1–8

God had promised as early as Eden that the day would come when sin would be conquered by the seed of the woman. He has now begun to take steps toward bringing this about. In our reading we see how God chose Abram from the land of Ur of the Chaldees and gave him directions to leave his people and go to a land God would show him. God made a covenant with Abram that He would be his God and the God of his children after him. He changed Abram's name to Abraham, since he was to be the father of many nations (17:5). From him would come a people so closely identified with God that those who cursed the children of Abraham would find themselves cursed by God and those who blessed them would find themselves blessed by God. And God promised that through the seed of Abraham all the families of the earth would be blessed!

If we did not know that God was here preparing the line through which He would some day send His Son, we would be completely unable to see how the family of one mere man, a man whose faith was sometimes very weak, could make such an impact on the world. But the faith of Abraham was kept alive through the generations that followed him and it lives today in the Christian church. What a heritage is ours as his children!

Our pride is not really in Abraham, our father in the faith, however. We boast in God's Son, born of Abraham's line. He is the Seed who was promised. He is the One in whom all the families of the earth are blessed. All the families? Yes, the blessing of Abraham comes upon all who hear the gospel and respond in faith. And where the gospel of his Seed, God's Son, is poured out, blessing spills over and touches for good even the unbelieving. Western civilization with its many benefits and accomplishments is what it is because of the enlightenment of the gospel working in its people through the centuries. God's people are light, and that light reaches the remotest corners of the earth.

We may tell our Jewish friends that we, like them, are children of Abraham. We are his spiritual heirs. We who believe in Christ as our Saviour and Lord are adopted into the family of Abraham according to God's covenant. They, too, may become heirs spiritually as well as physically. So may any who will come to God through faith in His Son.

We praise God for the unity of believers, as we all claim Abraham as father. We praise Him for Christ to whose coming Abraham looked forward and through whom we as well as Abraham have life eternal.

SARAH TRIES TO HELP GOD
Genesis 16:1–6

God had made it amply clear that He would cause Abraham to be the father of a great nation, as numerous as the stars of those Eastern skies or as the sands of the sea. Did Sarah disbelieve God? She would probably have denied that, but her belief did not extend to waiting for God. She became impatient and decided that He needed her help. So she offered her maid to be the mother of Abraham's son. In her stumbling faith Sarah was contriving a way to enable God to keep His promise.

How often we take into our own hands things that are the prerogatives of God alone! If not as blatantly as Sarah, yet in slightly shady ways, by covert means, we attempt to bring about God's purposes. In the church as well as in the home we hunt for short-cuts, for instant religion and 'easy believism.' God's plan is not to be rushed. There is an elegant, majestic walk about the eternal God. His plan may include years of waiting. He has lessons to teach us as we wait, lessons of faith and perseverance and hope.

'Mom, I don't see how you prayed seventeen years for me!' But the mother and the father had done just that. And who is to say that this was too long to wait for a son's salvation? It was God's timing. Through it He was accomplishing His purposes. He answered when those purposes had been accomplished. Praise His name!

THE SIGN OF THE COVENANT
Genesis 17:1–14

When God made formal agreement or covenant with Abraham to be his God and the God of his children after him, He gave a sign to mark them off from the world. That sign was circumcision. Adults entering into covenant with God were to receive this sign. And male children born into their families were to receive it likewise, because God was including them in His covenant (17:9–14).

As time went on it became clear that not all who had received this sign were demonstrating obedience to God which would show that they were His children. To these God said, 'Circumcise therefore the foreskin of your heart, and be no more stiff-necked' (Deuteronomy 10:16). He had to call them to repentance and—often through experiences of captivity or calamity—draw them back into fellowship with Himself.

God has given us today the sign of baptism which both adults who believe and their children are to receive, a sign involving not blood (since the shedding of the blood of the Perfect Sacrifice was accomplished at Calvary) but water (the cleansing by God's Word and Spirit). We are people set apart within God's covenant and baptism is the God-given outward sign of that distinction.

Is it not the same today as it was before Christ? Those who are bearing the outward sign of inclusion within God's family do not always show evidence of baptism into the death of Christ, with the newness of life that should follow. They often need to be called to repentance and new obedience. Sometimes God has to use gracious severity with us, too, to bring us back to Himself.

How is it with us? And with our children?

GOD KEEPS HIS PROMISE
Genesis 21:1–12

God had promised Abraham that he would make of him a great nation. The years came and went, years of waiting, sometimes in faith, sometimes in discouragement. Finally, when Abraham was a hundred years old and Sarah was long past the age of child-bearing, God granted them a son!

Sarah had laughed at the thought of the birth of a son. When he was born she even named him Laughter (Isaac). This was different from her scornful laugh when the angel announced she should bear this son! This was a laugh of joy at the keeping by God of His years-old promise. And Abraham made a great feast the day Isaac was weaned.

But all was not laughter in the home. There was the other mother and her son. Abraham had love for this son, too. The jealousy of Sarah, springing from her own decision to help God by offering Hagar to her husband, was like a knife in Abraham's bosom. How could he endure to see the discord in the home? And how could he bear to see Hagar and Ishmael sent away?

Oddly enough, God told Abraham to heed Sarah and send the bondwoman and her son away. God's purpose was not to be thwarted. It was the seed of the promise, the seed of the free-woman, who was to be the heir, not the seed of the bondwoman.

[43]

God was teaching lessons that men would not fully comprehend until He explained them centuries later through Paul. We today, Paul tells us, are the seed of Sarah, the freewoman, the seed of promise. We are spiritual children of Abraham in the great family of the faithful. We are in that company that is as the stars of the sky and the sands of the seashore for multitude!

That is why we, as the children of faithful Abraham, should glory in a salvation that is by faith. That is why we should not attempt to reduce our salvation to a system of bondage to works as did the Galatians. We should not act as though we are born of the slave woman!

PARENTAL LOVE AND GOD'S LOVE
Genesis 22:1–14

Abraham loved God. His love for God is seen from the time He first heard God's call to leave family and homeland and go into a far-away country, not knowing where. His love is evidenced through the long years of wandering. Abraham was a friend of God.

Abraham loved Isaac. Who does not love his own child, his flesh and blood? Especially, it might seem, does the parent who has been long childless, dote upon the child who finally is born. What if that child were born in fulfilment of a promise of God! What if that child were born when the father was one hundred years old and the mother ninety? Indeed, Abraham loved Isaac!

That dual love is what makes this scene on the mountain in the land of Moriah one of the most dramatic and tense in the whole range of historical literature! The eyes and sympathy of all readers rest with this father, knife in hand, and all wait for the impossible decision.

But Abraham's priorities were straight. His faith in God, proven in the past, did not waver now. If God demanded the sacrifice of his son, that he would make. His love for God, his trust in God, were unfaltering!

What was Abraham thinking? He may have been thinking, God will not let me do this. After all, He promised me a family in which all the nations would be blessed. He GAVE this son to me in fulfilment of that promise. Maybe He will intervene. Maybe He will raise this child from the dead. I do not know. I just know that He has commanded me to do this thing. So I will do it.

What an object lesson this is for us! God so loved that He, too, gave His Son. How great is our love for God? Is it greater than our love for our children? If He wants them in Africa is that all right with us? If we have to make the choice, will our choice be to serve our God or our children?

Jesus said, 'He that loveth son or daughter more than me is not worthy of me' (Matthew 10:37).

[45]

'ARRANGED MARRIAGES'
Genesis 24:1–9

A Chinese friend of ours was once asked whether hers had been an 'arranged marriage.' She laughed and replied, 'Yes! It was arranged by God.' In our culture parents do not ordinarily arrange marriages for their children. As Christian parents, however, we may have the confidence that God our Father arranges them according to His will. His arrangements are for the good of His children and for His own glory.

Abraham was concerned about the marriage of his son. He was probably particularly concerned about this marriage because of his confidence that God was doing a very special thing with his family. His concern was converted into action. He made provision that his son's marriage be 'in the Lord.'

It would not be possible for us to follow the course Abraham followed. But there *are* things we can do that the Lord may use in arranging a Christian marriage for our children.

Being a happily married couple in the Lord is of paramount importance. Setting within our children the goal of having a marriage like ours flows from this. In addition it is important to provide positive, and, when needed, negative teaching about sex and marriage and interpersonal relationships. It is important, also, to provide the climate for the development of Christian companionship at home, at church, and if possible at school. In general we need to strive to maintain in the home a relationship of confidence and respect so that parental advice concerning marriage plans will be sought and accepted.

Are we who are parents praying now that God will arrange the lives of our children including their marriage? What concern are we showing about other young people in our church family as they approach adult years? God uses means as He arranges marriages. When young people see our marriage are they encouraged to seek for themselves a marriage that is in the Lord?

EARLY TRAINING
Exodus 2:1–10

Abraham's great-grandson, Joseph, was sold into Egypt. In the providence of God his family, the Israelites, lived there as slaves to the Egyptians some four hundred years. Then it was that the boy Moses was born.

Hollywood versions of the youth of Moses might lead us to believe that he was unaware through his younger days of his Hebrew parentage. But the account in Scripture indicates otherwise. The mother of Moses was a faithful mother in Israel who trained her children thoroughly and well so that they knew who their God was and what He had done for them in the past.

It is believed that in the days of Moses babies were not weaned until perhaps five years of age. In this case we can well see how the faith of

Moses became firmly fixed upon his God before he was taken to live in the palace-home of the Pharaoh's daughter.

Then it is easy to understand verse 11 where we are told that when Moses was grown he went out to his brothers and saw their misery. He knew they were his brothers and as he grew older he wanted to see how they really fared. It is not fanciful to imagine that while he was growing up in the court he had a gnawing nostalgia for the simple though arduous life among people who were different because they knew and served Jehovah.

It is being demonstrated that a child's environment in his earliest years has a tremendous effect upon his development. From this springs the trend toward having the new-born baby sleep in his mother's room in the hospital. Likewise, breast-feeding and physical closeness in infancy are being recognized more and more as significant factors in the development of good emotional health.

Are we being as careful that our children should learn the love and discipline of God through us even from their mother's womb?

GOD GIVES HIS LAW
Exodus 20:1–17

Moses grew up. God used him to deliver His people from the bondage of the Egyptians and bring them to the mountain called Sinai. God today delivers the people, whom He chose before the foundation of the world, out of the bondage of sin into the freedom which is in Christ.

At Sinai God gave, in the form of a code of ten laws, standards for conduct which are man's guide for living. The Ten Commandments have been called a transcript of the divine nature. They are a revelation to man of what it means to be righteous! To be completely in harmony with God one would have to keep His law perfectly.

Of course we cannot do this. But God, since He could not have fellowship with unrighteousness, sent His Son to keep that law perfectly so that we by faith might be righteous in God's sight. It was not enough that Christ bore in His death the penalty for our transgression of this law! He kept this law perfectly so that we might by faith have His righteousness credited to our account.

Today the Decalogue still stands as a guide for our living. Not only this, but it stands as a guide for the teaching of our children. Let us not pass over verse 10 as a mere appendage to verse 8. It is also an amazingly strong enunciation of the principle of parental responsibility! The father is responsible for the conduct of his whole family, even the guests whose unexpected arrival might 'keep us from going to church.' God has made the father responsible for the honoring of His day by all the household.

And this goes for training in the whole law as well. How we should pray for fathers in Israel in their task!

GOD'S PEOPLE MAKE THE FIRST CHURCH
Exodus 35:22–29

God ordered a tabernacle to be constructed for His worship. Sometimes we get lost in the details for the building of the tabernacle and later the temple. We lose sight of some of the gems we find in chapters like this.

Men and women who were willing-hearted and wise-hearted brought the God-given raw materials and with them employed their God-given talents to make a beautiful place in which to worship Him. Read the whole chapter when you are able and note the recurrence of this theme.

God loves beauty. He was the first Artist. Ever since creation He has been continuously making a sunrise and a sunset, circling the world ceaselessly with a beauty that declares His glory! For God is glorified in beauty. And He has made us, who were made in His image, to be creative, too. Do we develop our gifts? Do we give Him the glory for them? Do we use our gifts as opportunity arises in His service?

Our homes should be as beautiful as we can make them, not extravagantly but simply beautiful. The parallel between the home in which the family lives and the church in which the family of God gathers requires that we regard each as a special place. What a happy place when the members are willing-hearted and wise-hearted as they apply their talents to creating a tangible beauty as well as a spiritual beauty!

WOMEN'S RIGHTS
Numbers 27:1–8

Normally, God has provided for meeting a woman's needs of a material and protective nature, and indeed of a spiritual nature, through the man who is her father or her husband. Part of the onerous task of the man is this care he has for the members of his family. He who does not shoulder this burden is worse than an infidel. When no member of a family is available to take care of these needs the church is to accept this responsibility. This is all in God's plan for those He loves.

Scripture does not declare to us a God who is insensitive to the humanness of women and to their needs, whether spiritual or temporal. Women are people. There is not male and female before the Lord as far as the soul is concerned. And here we see written into the laws of the Jewish nation that if there were no sons the father's inheritance should be given to his daughters.

Note how graciously Moses and Eleazar and God Himself responded to the five women who stood at the door of the tabernacle and made their speech. A careful reading of the Old Testament does not support the accusation that women under Old Testament laws were mere chattels! Not only in Proverbs 31 and the Song of Solomon, but even hidden among these sometimes tedious listings of laws in the Pentateuch, we see how God regarded the one who like Adam was made in His image and who was designed to be a helper appropriate for Adam.

GOD SPEAKS TO PARENTS
Deuteronomy 6:1–9

This is perhaps the most appropriate passage in Scripture for study concerning the godly home. It covers two main thoughts. First, the parent himself needs to be completely devoted to God. Second, the parent needs to provide a totally Christian environment for his children. These are the twin goals toward which we need to be striving in the Lord.

Within the parent there is to be a harmony of doctrine and life, with no contradiction, no hypocrisy. God's statutes are to be known and believed and they are to be kept. God, the one true God, is to be worshipped, loved and obeyed.

Then, what we know we are to impart to our children. Those truths which God has revealed are to be shared with our children. *Share* is a weak word here. We are to indoctrinate our children! We are to do it diligently. Not only are we to teach them, which suggests a more formal presentation, but we are to talk freely with them about God our Father morning, noon and night. Every moment our conversation must acknowledge God, as we take a walk, sit at the table, whatever we do.

It must be evident to the neighbors that we know God. The Jews literally placed a copy of the law on their wrists, and on their forehead and at the posts of the door. Some orthodox Jews still retain this custom. But we may be sure that God, who knows the heart, is concerned here to emphasize His desire that His law is to be so much a part of us that we are never without a consciousness of it, and that its principles are reflected in all our actions for the world to see.

The more it becomes evident that the god of the secular world is Man, the more Christian parents should be questioning whether the secular school meets the requirement laid out here for parents to provide a totally Christian environment. What a challenge is Deuteronomy 6 to us as we examine both our own commitment and the environment we are providing for our children!

QUESTIONS AND ANSWERS IN THE HOME
Deuteronomy 6:20–25

Did you ever realize that God spoke to Moses about the importance of communication in interpersonal relationships? 'When thy son asketh thee . . . thou shalt say . . .' (6:20,21).

God is pleased to have us respect each other in the home. He is pleased to have us recognize that we are able to help one another. So we are to communicate to one another our questions, our fears, our anxieties, our problems, as well as our joys! And He is pleased to have us listen to those around us, really listen, and then in utter seriousness and concern answer in truth and love.

When our son asks us why we are zealous to keep God's day holy, we should be happy to remind him that God, in His grace, has brought us out of a life of sin by His Son and that we want to please Him by our obedience. He has given us rules for living 'for our good always, that he might preserve us alive' (6:24). When we keep His law it shall be 'our righteousness.' We cannot hope to achieve salvation by keeping it perfectly. Only Christ could do this for us. But we love God and we *want* to be righteous and obedient!

When we become parents we are driven more and more to God's Word so that we may be thoroughly equipped to answer the questions of our children in accordance with God's truth. We need daily to search the Scriptures and become workmen who need not to be ashamed. But a parent endears himself to his child when he is willing to admit that he does not know all the answers or that his own faith sometimes needs bolstering, too!

Lord, help us to be honest and respectful in

our communications in the home; help us not to shut off questions our children ask; help us to treat our children gently! Lord, give us answers that honor You. And give us humility when we do not know the answers.

REBELLIOUS SONS
Deuteronomy 21:18–21

There are some things in the Bible we might wish were not there. This account is one such. This is an example of what the liberal theologian points to when he refers to the wrathful God of the Old Testament. But the conscientious, honest Christian has to be willing to face all parts of Scripture and to strive to see what God wants him to learn, even from a portion like this.

First of all, we are not to suppose that in our days we are at fault for not stoning rebellious children! This regulation was for Israel, the theocracy. This was one of the laws that was limited in its application to the time when Israel was a political unit under God and was governed according to special laws that God gave the nation.

However, we can learn from this law three things for our own day. First, the father is responsible for training his child in respect and obedience, in facing up to acts of defiance and disobedience and dealing with them. Second, the sin of stubbornness and rebellion against God-given parental authority is *VERY* serious. And third, the

[55]

Christian community should be concerned with the life-style of all its children.

Rebellion against a parent is rebellion against the God who says, 'Children, obey your parents in the Lord' (Ephesians 6:1). Rebellion is not to be considered a stage through which the normal youth will pass as he enters into his own independent life-style. It is true that a young person needs to mature into an adult who is controlled by self under God, instead of, as in his younger years, by parents under God. But this maturing and developing, and firm but respectful taking of the reins into his own hands from the hands of his parents, need not be rebellion!

God certainly has a lesson for us here. Let us heed it.

SOME RULES ABOUT MARRIAGE
Deuteronomy 24:1–5

In the beginning God declared that a man and a woman were to become one flesh in marriage. Their union was until death and no one was to separate them. Then there was the Fall. It affected marriage just as it affected all other aspects of life.

So it was that God, one might say, gave reluctant permission for divorce, knowing that often sinful men and women were making a hell for themselves and for their children as they tried to maintain a home where there was no love.

The type of divorce that was permitted in Old

Testament days was a total breaking of the bond. And remarriage to another person was permitted in that case. However, the original couple could not resume their marriage relationship at a later time.

As the Lord Jesus tells us, in the beginning this was not so. He laid down for us today a much stricter regulation concerning marriage (Matthew 19:3–9; Mark 10:2–9). But the Christian should understand these verses in Deuteronomy and their place in the history of God's people.

This, you see, was really a sign of God's grace. And verse five is another sign! What a tender verse this is! How like God it was to provide for the new bride a year in which her husband was to be freed from duty in war and business responsibilities in order to be able to stay at home and cheer up his wife! This was a long honeymoon! This is surely in line with the general tenor of Scripture that a man should love his wife as himself and treat her gently. After all, that is how the Lord, the Husband, loves and treats His Bride the Church.

THE PARENTS' TESTIMONY
Joshua 4:19–24

After commenting upon Deuteronomy 6:20–25 we might well pass over this section. But that was Moses. This is the testimony of Joshua.

After Moses died God's people were led into

the Promised Land by Joshua. Under his brave leadership they passed through the Jordan River in a fashion that reminds us of the way in which God enabled Moses to lead them through the Red Sea.

As they were passing through the river they took from the river bed twelve stones, one for each tribe. They placed these on the shore on the far side, in accordance with the command of the Lord.

Why did God command this strange thing? He did it to form the basis of training for the children not yet old enough to understand the miracle God was performing, yea, even for the children not yet born. He did it as a vehicle for the testimony of the parents.

The children would see the heap of stones. They would say, 'What do these stones mean, Dad?' (What does the bread mean, and the wine, in the Lord's Supper?)

And the parent would be able to say, 'God brought His people through this rushing river over to the Land of Promise. He preserved us. He cared for us. He is our God!' (God brought His people out of sin and sorrow. The bread and the wine represent the body and blood of His own Son, crucified for us, to make atonement for our sins. He so loved us! He is our God!)

How good is God to save and take care of His people! And how good He is to give parents the opportunity to bear testimony unto their children concerning His grace!

MAKING SURE
Joshua 24:13–28

God had been good. And now His people had been brought from the bondage of the Pharaoh and the perils from man and beast and nature during their wilderness wanderings. They were in the land He had promised.

How careful Joshua is to set before them the seriousness of a recommitment to God at this time! How careful he is to point out the exclusiveness of worship to Jehovah! Joshua is positive that he himself desires to serve God with his house. But he does not want the people, like unthinking sheep, to make too easy a commitment by automatically following his example and speaking glib words.

It *is* a big, serious, exclusive step to set up a household with God as its foundation! He *is* a jealous God. Are we fully aware of the implications of Joshua's words, 'As for me and my house, we will serve the Lord' (24:15)? Are we sure we will obey His Word even if this means that we must deny ourselves certain things the world calls our rights—time, pleasure, money? Are we sure that we are ready to devote ourselves to His service and obey Him?

O God, give us the conviction that led Joshua to his declaration for You! And then give us the strength of Your Holy Spirit to enable us to follow through in our commitment.

A MOTHER IN ISRAEL
Judges 5

Deborah and Barak are singing antiphonally, leading their people in the praise of God for His victory over the hosts of Sisera. Their strangely beautiful song is a tribute to the God who gave them the victory.

There are three women in this song—Deborah, Jael, and the mother of Sisera. First there is Deborah, the mother in Israel who arose at a time of desperate need. Why did God call Deborah from her home to assume this leadership and rally the forces of her people? Were there no men? Did God choose her so that we might see that it was He who won the victory in the way of His choosing, with the leader of His choosing?

Then there was Jael, who slew the enemy when he came, parched and weary, to the very door of her tent. Again God used a woman in His battle. Was this to shame the enemy before the Israelites? Was it to encourage women that they, too, may be instruments in the hand of God?

Then there was the mother of Sisera, a heathen woman who waited in vain for the return of her son, inventing for herself peaceable and safe reasons to explain his delay. Why did God include her in His Book? There is surely something more important than the poignancy of her language, although we are struck by the way in which the destruction of the enemies of God is crystalized in the experience of this woman. The grief of the mother of Sisera symbolizes the grief of unbelief and hopelessness of the person outside God. And God is pointing out, obliquely, the universality of the mother-heart and the dignity of personality. As we read this we see striking evidence that man is made in the image of the Creator and that every human being is special.

The song concludes:

Thus let all Thine enemies perish, O Lord:
But let those who love Him be like the rising
of the sun in its might (5:31 NASB).

The verse and chapter end, 'And the land was undisturbed for forty years,' forty years of peace in an Israel which had known so much of bloodshed! And the Lord used two women to bring about this peace.

DISHONOR YOUR FATHER?
Judges 6:11–16 and 25–32

We rejoice in the Bible's emphasis on the family. We recognize that God requires us to obey and honor parents. They are set up by Him as a channel for our nurture and blessing.

But sometimes parents do not know God. Sometimes to follow them is to dishonor God. This provides a dilemma for many young people today whom God has brought out of an atmosphere of unbelief into faith through His Son.

In the Promised Land all was not peace for

God's people. Soon after the time of Deborah they were oppressed by the Midianites. Young Gideon was given by God the task of saving his people from this ungodly tyranny. In verse 25 God tells him to destroy the altar 'which thy father hath.' He is to defy his father, to cut the family bonds of natural affection and filial regard by symbolically destroying the religious life of his father and his household.

Gideon was understandably fearful of this. He did the job at night so that he would not be detected in the act. But this could not be kept from his father. His father learned of the deed and so did all the neighbors.

God is full of surprises. When the neighbors demanded that the father Joash should punish his son by death for this deed he turned the tables on them. He rebuked them for pleading for a god! 'Let him plead for himself,' he retorted (6:31).

Who knows but that God might repeat this event as young people today take a stand for Him against the false faith of their fathers? The gracious Lord may very well use a loving zeal and testimony to unify the whole family in Himself. This should be our prayer for young people in similar circumstances. And what about us and our parents?

HOW SHALL WE TRAIN THIS CHILD?
Judges 13:8–14

Samson was another one like Gideon to whom God entrusted the task of delivering His people from oppressors. Samson's parents were told by God that their son would have this special task. What was their response? They asked God to teach them what they should do to this child who would be born (13:8). Then again the father asked, 'How shall we order the child, and how shall we do unto him?' (13:12).

Do we hope for a child? Do we await a child? Do we have a child? This is a prayer we should be praying every day: 'Lord, what shall we do to this child? Help us to train and teach him, to love and discipline him for You.' The child is from Him. Our child might not have a spectacular task to perform such as God gave to Samson. But every child is special in God's sight and has a certain sphere of influence where he alone may bear testimony for the Lord. We need to be taught by God's Word and Spirit how to train him.

Parents feel the pressure on every side from books on child-psychology and child-rearing. Some of them give helpful insights and may be read with profit. Many, however, are based upon a completely humanistic view of the nature of man and his needs. Unless we are extremely cautious we may be taken in by the logical-sounding advice they offer. We need ever to be reading critically and weighing what we read!

How grateful we may be to God that He has not left us without a *Manual for Possessors of New Babies.* We have His book of directions, based upon His knowledge of the nature of His creatures and their needs. When the Bible seems to run counter to contemporary views we need the humility and faith to accept it as our basis for training our children.

Furthermore, we need daily prayer for the wisdom and strength to apply divine principles, even when they may be challenged by educators, other parents and friends, and the children themselves.

O God, this is a frightening task You have given us. Show us the way.

A WOMAN'S GIFTS
Judges 13:15–25

Psychologists have noted basic differences between men and women. God, in His plan for the home, designed it this way. Two right gloves do not make a pair. Man and woman were made similar in order that they might have a deep understanding and communion. But God made them with certain differences in order that they might form a strong union. This is the genius of communion and completion.

In today's reading we see an example of a gift frequently given to women. Men are observed often to become easily discouraged, but to women has been given the gift of a faith or optimism or vision which enables them to provide encouragement in time of need.

Manoah is terrified. He says, 'We shall surely die because we have seen God' (13:22). In calm faith his wife answers, 'If the Lord were pleased to kill us, he would not have received our burnt offering or told us all these things about our son.'

This reminds us of an incident in the life of Martin Luther and his wife. Luther was very much discouraged with the way he felt the Lord's work was declining. He sat at his desk, depressed and gloomy. Suddenly he became aware of someone at the door. It was his wife, Katy. He was startled to see her standing there, dressed in somber black. 'What is the matter,' he asked. 'Is someone dead?' 'Yes,' answered Katy seriously, 'God is dead.' With gentle humor Katy had preached a sermon on faith to her preacher-husband, a sermon he would never forget.

Woman, are you exercising this gift of encouragement when your husband needs it so desperately? Husband, have you thanked God for a wife whose faith shines clear in the face of illness and poverty, as well as the day-by-day discouragements?

I HAVE SEEN A WOMAN
Judges 14:1–4

According to the brief account of this incident, Samson became infatuated with a woman whom he did not even know. Although he realized that God wants His people to marry within the faith he wanted this heathen woman for himself.

From the brief account, also, it appears that Samson had little desire to honor his parents. They would have opposed the marriage. But he went against the will of God and of his parents, and further showed his disregard for his father and mother by ordering them very abruptly to go and get her for him!

Samson was guilty before God on two counts: marrying outside the faith, and dishonoring his parents. Nothing that occurred later on excuses this action of Samson. No rationalizing can discount this sin.

But God's secret will is unfathomable. And it was running under all that happened, just as it was in the devilish betrayal of our Lord by Judas. And God even here was paving the way for the downfall of the Philistines, enemies of God and of His people; just as He was, in the case of Judas, fulfilling His plan for Satan to be cast out!

We cannot know God's secret will. When, after an interval of time, it becomes clear that He has been working mysteriously, we are amazed. But His revealed will, his command set forth so clearly in His Word, is not mysterious. And this is what should concern us. Obedience to His revealed will is what He requires of His people. This undoubtedly includes the matter of marriage within the faith.

Sometimes a young person in sinful rebellion marries outside the faith, as did Samson. And sometimes in such marriages the unbelieving partner comes to the Lord! This we must recognize as an act of God's grace in the face of sin! His grace does not justify the sin, it overrules it. So we must never completely despair in the face of a mixed marriage, whether it is our own or that of our child. God is able. And God is very gracious.

IN-LAWS
Ruth 1:1–13

The in-law problem can be a blight in the family. God has given us a rule that at marriage we leave (not just physically but from the point of view of authority and loyalties) our parental home and become one with our mate in establishing a new home. Often it is a failure to understand and work out practically the implications of this Biblical principle that is the root of marital problems.

This is easy to understand, is it not? Parents have had a consuming interest in their children. They have striven to provide for them, train them, help them on for some twenty years, perhaps. Now they are asked to keep hands off, to relinquish their authority and interest. Now the family group is broken up!

What can we say to the parent? We can say that this is what we were doing all the time, namely, training the child to go on his own and set up his own family unit. His success in this venture, accomplished now without our tutelage, is an indication of our good training. God says that man and wife are one. We can pray and be ready to help when called on, but never may we mar that oneness.

What can we say to the young couple? We can remind them, too, of the years when the parents were devoted almost entirely to their care. We can remind them to put themselves in the place of their parents who are facing a new and in some ways empty period.

But we must warn the young couple to be strong. Their marriage, their family life, must not be spoiled by interference from the older generation. The husband as head of the home must deal with this matter. Firmly, openly, and in a Christian manner he must discuss problems. He must not let his wife be caught between loyalties.

Is this sound Scripturally? Test it. It involves honesty, selfless love, a regard for God's government of the home.

Ruth and Naomi may seem to have been a different case, because the man they both loved was dead. But such a relationship must needs have originated in the years when he was living! And as we shall see later, their good relationship was maintained even when another man entered! Naomi's strength and Ruth's loyalty brought peace into this new home too. We may believe that their relationship with God was the key to their harmony.

WEDDING MUSIC?
Ruth 1:14–22

We have grown used to hearing the words of Ruth at a wedding:

> Intreat me not to leave thee,
> Or to return from following after thee:
> For whither thou goest, I will go;
> And where thou lodgest, I will lodge:
> Thy people shall be my people,
> And thy God my God (1:16).

These are utterly appropriate words for the Christian couple to employ as a pledge of fidelity to each other on the day of their marriage.

But the speaking of these words by a widow to her husband's mother is a moving and even strange phenomenon. And yet, should it be strange? Naomi and Ruth both loved the same man. In adversity they were drawn closer together. And they had the same God!

It is an ugly thing for jealousy to exist between a man's mother and his wife. It is foolish of them to vie for his affection and time, and to compete for his admiration of their cooking! Jealousy is both ugly and pernicious, a source of tension and unhappiness for the two women and for the man himself.

The mother must pray for grace to see another take first place in her son's life. She must remember her own husband and the need they had to build a separate unit early in their marriage. She needs to remember God's plan: two people made one. She needs to find new ways to express her affection to her son, quiet, unobtrusive ways that do not threaten his wife.

The wife needs to be patient, humble. She needs to admit it if her mother-in-law makes better pie-crust! What a 'big' person she would prove herself to be if she were to become pupil of the more experienced cook and so improve her skills and please her husband! And the wife needs to project herself into the day when her own son will go away with another woman.

As for the man, he needs to be a real diplomat, tactfully dealing with these two women in love and firmness. He needs to be strong. And he needs to be sure that his priorities are right so that he protects his chosen one against anyone who might attempt to usurp her place—even his own mother, or hers!

GRANDMOTHER NAOMI
Ruth 4:9–22

When Naomi had returned to Bethlehem, widowed and her sons deceased, she disclaimed her given name. 'Call me Mara, for the Almighty hath dealt very bitterly with me,' she said (1:20).

In the providence of God, the story of Naomi and her devoted daughter-in-law had a happy ending. A well-to-do man, Boaz, became the husband of the young widow from Moab. And a son was born to them whom they called Obed. No longer needed Naomi to be called Mara! Now the townswomen point out that Ruth is better to her than seven sons (4:15). And now she rejoices in a grandchild for whom she is given special responsibility.

In our culture it is difficult to understand the relationships that existed in this home. But there is no evidence that there was a problem and we cannot go further than the text. All we can say from the information that we have is that this was a home where there was love and understanding. Naomi, who had suffered so much in younger years, had found her God faithful. The death of husband and sons was tragedy. But then came a new life—a life in the line of the Messiah!

Naomi's rejoicing is a special tender note in Scripture. We often point out the joy of motherhood and speak apprehensively of the days when the children will be gone. But in that 'empty nest' period we may be blessed by God when grandchildren appear and we are privileged to have another special function in God's economy, because grandparents have a very precious place in the lives of children. And they receive more joy than they give!

Tragedy may come, but we must not despair as the world does. Our God is faithful through all the years!

THE TRIANGLE
1 Samuel 1:1–8

God never approved polygamy. He ordained in the beginning the marriage of one man to one woman. Jesus explained to us that for a while God permitted divorce for reasons other than adultery because of the hardness of men's hearts. It appears that for the same reason He tolerated polygamy. But this was not His plan for a happy marriage. It repudiated His analogy of His own relationship to His Bride, the Church, which He pictures for us in both Old and New Testaments.

Elkanah dearly loved Hannah. But their marriage was marred by the presence of Peninnah in the home. Hannah's distress was accentuated because she was barren whereas Peninnah had borne children to Elkanah.

What a poignant verse! 'Her adversary also provoked her sore, for to make her fret, because the Lord had shut up her womb' (1:6). Childlessness would have been difficult enough to bear without the taunts of another wife in the home. Even the reassurance of Elkanah could not assuage her grief.

God's way is the best way, the gracious way. His pattern is the path of peace and love and personal fulfilment. The only triangle in the home must be the triangle whose points are the man, the woman, and God. This kind of triangle assures a complete marriage, a marriage in accordance with the plan of God from the beginning.

BELIEVING PRAYER
1 Samuel 1:9–18

We have noted Hannah's deep distress. She was childless and she was taunted by another wife who had borne children. She went to the only One to whom she could go, that is, to God. She knew that He could help her. There was no mouthing of words or vain repetition in her prayer. Her zeal and earnestness led the priest to suppose, for the moment, that she was drunk. What a commentary on the prayer life at that time! Eli wasn't used to people praying like that.

Would a pastor today be surprised to see a barren woman pray like that for a child? Might he not think she was on drugs or fanatical?

God gave comfort to Hannah when she prayed. She knew He had heard her prayer and she believed that He would heed her request for a son. 'And her countenance was no more sad' (1:18). We who may be inclined to look condescendingly upon Old Testament believers as unenlightened people, not possessing the gift of the Holy Spirit in New Testament fulness, should observe the example of Hannah. She prayed. She prayed with all that was in her. And when she prayed she had the faith to believe that God had heard.

'Let him ask in faith,' says James, 'nothing wavering. For he that wavereth is like a wave of the sea driven with the wind and tossed. For let not that man think that he shall receive anything of the Lord' (James 1:6,7).

Lord, we do believe. Help Thou our unbelief!
(Mark 9:24).

AN ANSWER TO PRAYER
1 Samuel 1:19-28

The child Samuel was an evidence that God answers prayer. How much this answer meant in
that home and land! His very name means 'asked
of God.'

But what about the hasty promise that Hannah
made to God in the urgency of her requesting,
or rather beseeching Him for a son? For perhaps
five years Hannah had the joy of caring for her
son. When the time came for her to give him
up, would she change her mind? No, she had
been preparing him for serving God in a special
way. This child, like Moses, was trained by
his mother in those earliest years to know God.
Samuel was taught to be willing to leave a
loving home and go to the tabernacle to serve
God.

The time came all too quickly. Hannah took
him there and left him, the child she had waited
for so long and prayed for so earnestly! He had
been made aware of his special task and function.
'And he worshipped the Lord there' (1:28).

Some of us lesser Hannahs have prayed that
the Lord might see fit to use our children in a
special way in His service. Have we followed
through and prepared them for God's work by
our faithful instruction in His truth? Have they

seen in us the joy of serving God? And if He does see fit to use them in some special way, will they be ready to say Yes? Will we be ready to let them go?

A PRAYER OF PRAISE
1 Samuel 2:1–10

What a prayer burst from the lips of Hannah at this time! God's ways were well known to her. He was sovereign. He had the power to set up and put down. He alone was holy. He was the God of all knowledge.

Men ought to come to God and render Him what is His due—honor, obedience, love. Hannah knew in her own heart what God would do. And she bowed to acknowledge Him and to praise Him as readily as she had pled to Him for a son.

We pray for the healing of a loved one. When he is healed do we thank God? When he is not healed do we still praise God for enabling us to accept His ways which are inscrutable but good?

We pray for the salvation of a parent, a child, a friend. Do we thank God when He regenerates this soul? If He tarries do we wait patiently for Him?

We pray for provision at a time of financial need. Do we glorify Him for meeting this need? Or for never letting us get to the position where such an acute need is ours?

'Were not ten cleansed?' asked Jesus. 'Where are the nine?' (Luke 17:17).

SONS OF THE PRIEST
1 Samuel 2:11–26

Satan often works in the homes of Christian leaders! What a victory for his side when their children dishonor God. How sad when the very work of the Lord sometimes is the cause, at least in the eyes of the world, of the rebellion of sons! How sad when the father is too much occupied with the work of 'the church' to take time to train his own children in the ways of the Lord!

While Samuel was ministering before the Lord in an honorable way, Eli's own sons were committing sacrilege. We cannot categorically blame parents for the negligence or sin of their sons. The sons themselves are accountable. But in this case God's Word tells us plainly that Eli did not restrain his sons as they were growing up (3:13). His reprimand in 2:23–25 was too late. Isn't this a sin of which our permissive generation is guilty?

The Christian father, particularly if he is engaged specifically in God's work, experiences real tension. How should he apportion his time? On the one hand, there are the needs of the people of God and of a dying world; on the other hand, there are the needs of his own family. The days seem so short. His time and strength are limited. It requires of him real grace and wisdom to set priorities properly and great understanding on the part of his family to accept his decision.

How much do we as God's people pray for the special servant of the Lord and his family? Do we limit our demands upon him when they might cut into his time with his loved ones? Are we courteous enough to include his wife and children in invitations when it is appropriate? And when necessary do we ever so gently point out to him his need to reassess his apportionment of time?

THE FATHER'S PROBLEM
1 Samuel 2:27–36

What, specifically, was Eli's problem? The twenty-ninth verse tells us that he honored his own sons above God. Do these words describe any Christian parents today? Do we ever pamper our children? Do we ever withhold punishment from them in spite of God's instruction to us to train them up in the way they should go? We want them to have fun, happiness, ease, comfort, popularity, things, things, things . . . And if this means we yield when it comes to insisting that they be obedient to God . . . ? And if this means we decrease our offering to God this week because son needs a new bicycle . . . ?

Sometimes we figure out so carefully that we

will not give our child an overdose of religion because that's what happened to the son of a friend of ours and he threw it all over! We won't *insist* he go to church *EVERY* Sunday because he might grow to hate it. We do not trust God to the extent of obeying Him implicitly and leaving the rest to Him. We are honoring our child more than we are honoring God.

When she was still very young one of our daughters said to her mother, 'I love you very much, mother. But I love God more than I love you.' What a tribute this declaration was! What a confession! It is difficult to know just how much the child could understand what she was saying, but her words were very precious to the mother. It was a real challenge, in fact. The mother wondered then and she wonders now, Could I say that to my daughter? Could I say, 'I love you very much, daughter, but I love God more than I love you'?

GOD SPEAKS TO A YOUNG MAN
1 Samuel 3:1–21

God did not often come in a personal way to speak to men in Samuel's days. His word was 'precious' and there was no 'open vision' (3:1). Nor was there, either, a Bible for sale at the Supermarket.

And the young Samuel had no previous experience of being addressed by God. But the Lord did speak to him. This is beautiful. God does speak to men. There is no age barrier on His part, either. Or sex barrier! He speaks to children as well as to adults. We should emphasize this to our children and the children of others as we tell them this story.

The other thing we must emphasize is the need of receptivity. Samuel's training and devotion had prepared him for a confrontation with God. At Eli's prompting he readily responded, 'Speak, Lord, for thy servant heareth' (3:9).

In our day God speaks to us through the Bible. First, are we listening? Do we even know what He is saying? And then, does it sink in? Are we receptive? Do we really hear? Do we heed?

Samuel did hear and he did heed. He 'feared to show Eli the vision' (3:15). But he did. He told the priest the whole horrible thing. Samuel was to continue to speak that way from God to the people all of his life, even to warning King Saul about the bleating of sheep and the lowing of oxen (15:14)!

And God was with him and 'let none of his words fall to the ground' (3:19). God prospered his ministry.

Hannah's prayers, we may believe, were following him up to the day of her death!

SONS OF THE PROPHET
1 Samuel 8:1–9

With the sad story of Eli and his sons before us, it is a surprise to read of Samuel's own sons,

Joel and Abiah! We would think that having an object lesson on the results of parental permissiveness enacted before his eyes would cause Samuel to take heed and be especially careful in his own family. And it may have been that he was! Here God's Word does not give us any indication of neglect on Samuel's part. As we read also in the case of the sons of some of the kings, Samuel's sons are said plainly to have 'walked not in his ways' (8:3).

What do we say about this? And what lesson is here for us? First, of course, we apply ourselves to bringing up our children in the fear and admonition of the Lord. We seek to avoid the sins of Eli. We give ourselves to prayer that God will be gracious to us and to the children He has given us.

But we remember that the salvation of our sons is a matter of individual responsibility. And we remember that ultimately it is a matter of the grace of our Sovereign God.

And in times of stress when it seems as though our children are so slow to respond to God's free offer of salvation there are things we may learn. It may be that we are the ones who need to be turned inside out to see whether there is any wicked way in us. Maybe God is striking at our most vulnerable part in order that we may be renovated by His Spirit!

And through it all we must submit to His will and know that He is working out all things to the good of His people as a whole and to His own ultimate glory.

THE BABY
1 Samuel 16:1–13

Our children may be over-concerned about clothing and personal appearance. They may show more interest in their outward appearance than in the needs of the soul. So we quote to them the second half of verse 7, 'The Lord seeth not as man seeth; for man looketh on the outward appearance, but the Lord looketh on the heart.' We probably do not quote it often enough.

But there is something else in this passage. Even Jesse was looking at the exterior, the image, the position, when he brought only the older sons to Samuel. Young David, the shepherd boy, was summarily dismissed. Was it because he was a 'stupid' shepherd? Was it because he was 'the baby'?

One of the things of which we as parents must constantly be aware is not to dub our children, either openly or in our own minds, the 'first-born,' 'the middle child,' 'the baby,' 'the brain,' 'the red-head,' 'the beauty queen,' 'the clown,' 'the one with all thumbs'! Parents do much harm in actually playing up a minor characteristic of a child, placing him into a mold he may always have to struggle to break out of. We must not lose sight of the person who is behind the exterior. Once the label is on the bottle it is sometimes difficult to get it off, even if the content is changed. And by listing only one of the ingredients on the label we often lose sight of other much more significant ingredients.

There was a girl who was really very ugly in childhood because of a facial disfigurement. She was talented and had much ability, but whenever her achievements forced her into the public eye she withdrew from this activity and started from scratch in some other endeavor! The time came when through remarkable surgery she was rid of her deformity and was now regarded as truly beautiful. But she still thought of herself as ugly and recoiled from being in the public eye. It was a long difficult struggle for her to form a *new* self-image. In a similar way, it is possible for parents to give their children malformed pictures of themselves from which they may not be able to escape in later life.

When God warned us against making graven images He was talking about something else. But there is a sense in which we can make the same application in our home. We must seek to *know* our children. Then we must very cautiously seek to help them to deal with their weak points or physical or dispositional problems. We certainly must not contribute toward forming in them a low self-image to which they will feel compelled to conform. We need rather to encourage them to a confidence in what is possible for them to be in Christ, helping them to develop their gifts.

O God, keep us from the foibles of parents in not really allowing our children the freedom of developing into the kind of people they are capable of becoming by Your grace.

A WOMAN OF GOOD JUDGMENT
1 Samuel 25:2–35

The boy David had at length become captain of the bodyguard of the king, son-in-law of the king and a man highly respected in the court. But he was forced to flee the court for his life. He was not safe in the presence of jealous Saul.

David had met Nabal and requested from him food for himself and his men who were hiding from Saul in the wilderness of Paran. Nabal was surly and mean and, despite the good treatment his shepherds had received from David, he refused to help.

Abigail, Nabal's beautiful and intelligent wife, was aghast at her husband's dealing with David. Hastily she rode her donkey out to David in the mountain ravine bringing abundant provisions from the store of her wealthy husband.

David praised God for meeting his need through this gracious woman. And to her he said, 'May you be blessed for your good judgment and for keeping me from bloodshed this day' (25:33 NIV).

Abigail waited till morning to tell Nabal what she had done, because that night Nabal was 'in high spirits and very drunk' (25:36 NIV). Another evidence of her good judgment!

We know the rest. Nabal was dead within ten days. When the news of his death reached David he called for Abigail and she became his wife.

How good that this story is included in Scripture! Here is a woman like some today, a godly woman of many gifts who is married to a fool (as the name Nabal means—25:25 NIV). But she does not succumb to her lot. She lives above her bad marriage. She acts as a responsible woman, doing courageously but discreetly what she knows is right in the sight of the Lord.

When we talk about the headship of the husband and the submission of the wife, we need to be careful to place over against this principle of Scripture another one: the wife is first of all a woman of God and it is not required of her to kow-tow to a drunken fool and neglect her own relationship to God. She needs to develop her spiritual life and use her gifts in His service. She needs to be her own person, or rather, the person that the Lord has made her.

DAVID TAKES HIS NEIGHBOR'S WIFE
2 Samuel 12:1-14

Here is a picture of the holiness of God and His hatred of sin. Adultery, even the lustful look or feeling, is not just a blot on our record, it is a sin against God!

And knowing the sinful state of mankind since the fall, Christians should be on constant guard against the sins of sex. We should shun TV programs, movies, music, dress styles, light jesting that tend to bring forth lustful feelings in ourselves or in those in our company. This applies, too, to light treatment of the institution of marriage or humorous comments or stories about sex.

Nathan was a brave man to address David, now King of Israel, in the words of this parable. But, also, King David was a humble man to receive this rebuke as from God. And what a punishment! God regarded this matter very seriously. In us, who have received the completed revelation and the fulness of the Spirit, He regards this sin of adultery, and even the adulterous look, as being certainly as heinous. This is the teaching of this passage.

But God had other reasons for including this incident in His Book. It is a promise to us when we sin. The attitude which David manifested toward his sin is an example and inspiration. All of us fall. God would have us recognize our failures and come to him humbly in confession. He would have us receive His forgiveness and seek His power to resist temptation in the future.

PARENTAL HONESTY
2 Samuel 13:1–15

How could David the father, who had himself committed adultery, train his son in the proper relationship between men and women? He ran the risk of being told, 'Physician, heal thyself.' But as we note his profession of love for God's law in the Psalms and sacred history, we believe he must have trained his children in just this way.

Did he say, honestly, frankly, repentantly, 'Son, I made a mistake, I sinned. God was displeased. And I had much unhappiness. You must be sure to honor God in this aspect of your life.' Solomon's declaration concerning his father's teaching would lead us to believe that this is precisely what he did.

There are parents who never admit to their children that they do wrong. God wants us to be honest. He wants us to say, 'I sinned.' He wants us to say, 'Forgive me.' He wants us to covet the prayers of our children in the handling of improper feelings, stubborn sins, sticky situations.

Often we see, as David did, our own sins cropping up in our children. Just as we sometimes receive a jolt as we look in the mirror and see our own parent's face looking out at us, we also see our own selfishness, pride, jealousy, quick temper in the lives of our children.

What are we to do? Sometimes we say casually, 'He is just like me. I understand because I had that same problem.' We excuse sin in our children because to condemn them would be to condemn ourselves!

God demands honesty in parents. He demands that we treat sin as sin, whether it is in ourselves or in our children. Sin must be confessed and brought repentantly before the God who is willing to forgive through His Son. Of course we will put ourselves in the place of our children as they experience the same problems that we had. But both the honest confession of our own sins and our own repentance are what they need to observe in us. We cannot hide our sins from them! Let us not try to do so.

LOVE IN PERSPECTIVE
2 Samuel 18:1–33

What a sorrow it is for a parent to see his son, even an unruly son, come to grief! Certainly the honest father can feel with King David as he mourns over Absalom, even though this son was proud, ambitious, and rebellious.

David loved Absalom. The Bible states that forthrightly. The actions of David attest to it. But there was something faulty in David's love. It was not farseeing. It was not balanced by discipline. It was selfish. It was not in perspective. His love was an emotional, blinding sentiment. Someone has said: 'Love without discipline is sentiment. Discipline without love is tyranny.' David's love was not the *agape* love of Scripture.

Should a father turn in to the police his son who is found in possession of drugs? Should a parent pamper one child in the family who is having a bad influence over the others? Should a mother give in to a child to prevent a temper tantrum? Many other questions might be asked in the context of today. This story is very contemporary.

What a difficult thing to speak to a father in

the words of verse 6 of the next chapter: 'You have loved your enemies and hated your friends. For if Absalom had lived and all of your friends had died you would be well pleased'! But this was a just rebuke. And fathers and mothers, blinded by sentiment and lacking in godly courage, sometimes need to be admonished in such a way by their true Christian friends.

O God, make us tough to do Your will. Help us to keep our love in perspective.

PERMISSIVENESS
1 Kings 1:5–14

In 1 Kings 15:5 we are told that David did right in the sight of the Lord 'save only in the matter of Uriah the Hittite.' In general he set an excellent example to his people and his own family.

But from this distance of time and space it appears to the reader of Scripture that with his children David was long on love and short on discipline. We saw an indication of this in the case of Absalom. Now we see that the delicate balance of love and discipline which needs to prevail in child training was tipped away from the discipline in the case of Adonijah, too. This is clear from verse 6: 'His father had not displeased him at any time in saying, Why hast thou done so?'

We saw permissiveness in Eli. Here we see it in David. Is it present in our own home? Rules or guide-lines must be well-known in the home, rules that stem from God's own law. Children must be helped to obey God by the example of the parent and by positive training. When there is disobedience there must be correction! The child must make amends for the wrong he has done, when it is possible. He must seek forgiveness of the offended party and also of God. And he must experience punishment to underline the seriousness of sin. There is no place for permissiveness in the home that would honor God.

A difficult order for the parent? Yes, but essential. Someone has said that being a parent is not a popularity contest. The child to whom we say, 'Why have you done this?' *will* be displeased. If we seem to be repetitive in this as in other matters, it is because God's Word is repetitive. By narrative, exhortation, command, God would enforce upon us lessons in parenthood which we sorely need and of which we need to be reminded frequently.

Lord, help us to be worthy parents!

SOLOMON'S WISDOM
1 Kings 3:5–15

Unlike Solomon, Absalom and Adonijah did not follow in their father's ways. David was, despite his sin, a man of God, and if all of his sons did not emulate him, young Solomon certainly did.

Young Solomon was remarkably discerning. He knew the truth of the New Testament verse:

'The things which are seen are temporal; but the things which are not seen are eternal' (2 Corinthians 4:18). And he chose from God the treasures that are eternal. Considering his palatial home and regal upbringing this is especially remarkable.

If a child in our home had such a choice, what would his decision be? Would he choose as Solomon did or would the materialism of the world about him warp his judgment? Are we careful not to complain overmuch about small salaries, inflation, taxes, inadequate housing? Are we unconsciously driving our children to seek a life in which the possession of a good income is the all-important thing? Are we fostering in them a determination not to 'suffer' as we did or do?

We would be dishonest not to comment upon the wealth that God granted Solomon. Although he did not choose it, he was granted it. Archaeologists believe they have discovered his horse-stables. The Queen of Sheba came from afar not only to hear his wisdom but to see his wealth.

The connection between his wealth and his defection in his latter years cannot be determined. One thing is certain, the wisdom God granted at his request was not directed to his marital life. This area, so important for his own spiritual life and the influence of his family, was an area in which the head wisdom which he possessed was not put into practice!

The young Solomon with his wise choice is an example of what we should do. The older Solomon in his weakness is an example of what we should not do.

THE KING AND THE BABIES
I Kings 3:16–28

One of the decisions of King Solomon which has come down to us regards the treatment of a baby claimed by two harlots. What feeble attempts at happiness are pictured here in the desire to possess a child even if it would be reared without a father and in an environment of sin and disgrace! Both of these women, despite their sinfulness, had a regard for the life and care of the little one for whose existence one of them was responsible.

How many women there are today who are harder of heart than these harlots and seek not to possess a living child but rather to abort an unborn child! The low estimate of human life reflected in the modern 'slaughter of the innocents' is frightening to those who recognize life as God's creation and children as His gift.

Not only is abortion *sin*, it is *suicide* to the peace of mind of the woman. And it is impoverishing to the home, for children *are* special, wonderful, created in the image of God. Happy is the man whose quiver is full of them. And happy is the woman who has borne them to him.

Babies are to be regarded with great honor— even before birth! They are not to be trafficked in, experimented upon, destroyed! Do not suppose Solomon was ruthless in his sentence and was risking murder! He discerned the mothers' hearts before him and the horror his proposition would arouse. It was his knowledge of these women that led to his sentence. And the response was as he anticipated.

This story has a lesson for our own day which was not as relevant even five years ago. God's people should be working hard to alert our world to the consequences of the light view of human life that we see all around us! The gospel is the one chief weapon against abortion! And this weapon lies in our hands.

RESPECT
2 Kings 2:19–25

This is one of those portions of Scripture we might have a desire to read quickly and not think about too much. But God has put it there and we should try to learn His reason for doing so.

First of all we must note that a better translation of verse 23 employs the term 'young lads' rather than 'little children.'

Second, we must look at the context. Elijah was a prophet of God in a day when God's truth was being denied on all sides. God honored His prophet by using him to perform the miracle of dividing the Jordan. God took him to heaven in a chariot. Then his successor, Elisha, was also enabled to divide the Jordan and afterwards to heal the waters of Jericho.

It was then, as Elisha was walking along the road toward Bethel, that a gang of teenagers began to make fun of him. Elisha pronounced a curse on them, surely at the bidding of God, and God underlined His displeasure at the disgraceful treatment of His prophet (and thus of Himself) by sending out from the woods two bears who 'tare forty and two of them' (2:24). Notice, there is no evidence that they met their death at this time.

This punishment at first blush seems harsh. But it is really a striking picture of the unity of God with His people. It is an evidence that those who harm us are insulting our God. What is done, in fact, to the least of one of God's people is done unto Him.

The appellation 'bald-head' is often grasped upon and emphasized, as though it was purely because these youths were making fun of Elisha's bald head that they were punished. But that was a term of contempt in the East. Any word or behavior which would express reproach would have been equally heinous in the sight of God, because it would have been an affront to Him and to His prophet.

Young people are to respect their elders. This story tells us so. But we should be careful to see the more significant implications. Young people, as well as older ones, need to respect God Himself!

THE PROPHET'S CHAMBER
2 Kings 4:8-10

Do you own your own home? Or does God?

The practice of hospitality may be approached from many angles. This matter of God's ownership of us and all we call our own is one angle. The matter of demonstrating God's love to strangers is another. There is even that practical angle of placing ourselves in the position of entertaining angels unawares!

The Shunammite woman is called a 'great' woman, which means that she was a woman of some wealth. When God grants us means and enables us to have a home, how better can we say 'Thank You' to Him than by having a prophet's chamber? This is like a perpetual tithing of our home!

The Christian world seems to be recovering the art of hospitality to some extent. Independence, affluence, motels and cars all probably contributed to its disappearance. What has contributed to its rediscovery? The L'Abris, the Christian communes?

We are enjoined by God to show hospitality. We have noted some of the angles to the question. Now we ask, what does hospitality do for a home? To answer that is exciting. People, created in the image of God, are wonderful. Each one is unique. Hospitality is educational! Contacts with people from a variety of racial, cultural, socio-economic backgrounds broaden our horizons. As the door of our home is unlatched to visitors to our church, missionaries and casual visitors as well, our home is enriched. The visiting Korean doctor, the Brazilian pastor, the black professor—these leave memories and mold attitudes in parents and children alike.

And what a joy to supply the needs of these visitors! What a deep joy to know the inspiration and encouragement our gesture of friendship can mean to a lonely person!

'Inasmuch as ye have done it unto one of the least of these my brethren,' said our Lord, 'ye have done it unto me' (Matthew 25:40). The union of Christ with His people comes through here as we consider the Shunammite woman, even as it did yesterday when we read of the boys and the bears.

CHILDLESSNESS
2 Kings 4:11–17

Why do women want to have children? We could simply say, Because God made them that way in order that His plan for a growing and continuing world might be realized. But there are many facets of the nature of women that could be mentioned to show how He accomplishes His purpose.

Having a child is experiencing something which validates her womanhood.

Having a child is the fulfilment of a woman's relationship with her husband.

[95]

Having a child changes the character of the home, bringing new love, challenge, fun!

Having a child continues the family and enables it to reach out into the future.

Having a child enables a woman to engage in a role of mothering and nurturing for which she was especially equipped by her Creator.

Having a child enables a man and a woman to express in a magnificent way their God-given creativity.

Having a child enables a human being to extend beyond the confines of self!

When asked by the prophet what she would like, this woman chose to have a child. In her day there was the added hope among Hebrew people that one's child might be the promised Messiah! Today we too experience a suggestion of this hope as we dream that our child may become a person of importance in the world—maybe not in the front rank, but at least a person of outstanding influence!

How sad that a growing number of women declare themselves uninterested in having children! For some inconsequential reason they are cutting themselves off from that which gives a woman one of her greatest joys.

And really, this all comes basically from an ignorance of God the Creator who had a plan, a very good plan! O God, open our eyes to the magnificence of Your plan, in all its wonder. Help us to be able to communicate it, by our lives and our words, to a needy world.

A BEREAVED MOTHER
2 Kings 4:18-37

To be long childless, then to have a child, then to lose him! What a deep sorrow! But the Shunammite woman's faith did not waver. She did not sit down and mourn. She knew that the God who could give her this son could restore him to her if He so chose.

She asked her husband for a servant and a donkey. She saddled the donkey. Off they went at full speed to find her prophet-friend.

God gave Elisha the power to restore life to the lad. The mother fell at the prophet's feet and bowed herself to the ground in gratitude. Then she took up her son and went out.

God sometimes sees fit to take our children today. We do not expect Him to raise them from the dead. But we must be as sure of our God as this woman was. We must submit to His wise providence and bow down before Him. In the words of Job, 'The Lord gave, and the Lord hath taken away; blessed be the name of the Lord' (Job 1:21).

The God of Elisha and of the Shunammite woman is the living God, the God of resurrection. He is ever 'the Resurrection and the Life.' Do we have a son or daughter who is dead spiritually? O God, give us the faith and vigor of this woman 'to run' to You for the life of this dead child!

PRAYER FOR A SAFE JOURNEY
Ezra 8:21–32

Ezra and his people were embarking on a journey that was fraught with danger. He might have asked the king for a band of soldiers and horsemen to protect them against the enemy in the way. But he was ashamed to do so!

Often he had borne testimony to the keeping power of God. He had declared that God's hand is on all them for good who seek Him. And he had also declared that God's power and wrath are against all who forsake Him.

So Ezra and his people fasted and prayed to God to seek of Him 'a right way for us, and for our little ones, and for all our substance' (8:21).

What an easy thing to understand! It comes home to us in many ways. We claim that our God loves and protects us. We should be ashamed to worry or complain. Instead we should pray for His continuing strength and protection!

And what about our journeys? Our dangers are not likely to be foreign enemies. But accidents may befall us! Do we entreat our loving Father and 'seek of him a right way for us, and for our little ones, and for all our substance'? When we settle into the family car for a trip it is appropriate to bow together in prayer for the mercies of God on our trip.

In verses 31 and 32 we read, 'And the hand

of our God was upon us . . . and we came to Jerusalem.' Our God is faithful and powerful to protect us and to bring us at last to our Jerusalem.

ARROW PRAYERS
Nehemiah 2:1-8

Nehemiah was cupbearer before the king. He was generally cheerful, though one of a captive people in a foreign land. But this day he was sad. The king noticed and asked the reason. When Nehemiah told him the cause of his sorrow, the king enquired how he could help.

Don't you love that sentence at the end of verse 4? Nehemiah, standing before the royal throne, sent a prayer like an arrow straight to the throne above. 'So I prayed to the God of heaven.' The earthly monarch had asked what he could do to help. Nehemiah recognized the fact that his help ultimately must come from the King of kings! Standing right there in the court he prayed.

God immediately helped him to ask wisely. The king made a generous response. The rest of the book tells of the rebuilding of Jerusalem which was thereby made possible.

We need to be conscious, not only at crisis times like this, but moment by moment, that we may send prayers like arrows to the throne of God. He can always hear. And He can answer while we are yet praying.

Specific periods of prayer are important, but

[99]

when Paul says, 'Pray without ceasing,' one of the things he surely means is that we are to have constantly the cast of mind and heart which will make it quite natural for us to speak to God about anything (1 Thessalonians 5:17).

AN UNBELIEVER'S INFLUENCE
Nehemiah 13:23–31

Solomon, for all his wisdom, was led into sin through marriage with godless women. 'The foreign women caused even him to sin' (13:26 NASB). In this startling sentence God reaches back into history and uses Solomon as an example and warning. If Solomon, with all his wisdom, was made to sin by marriage with unbelievers, what can we expect from those who are less wise than Solomon? A woman of beauty and physical charm has often led a man into temptation which he could not resist. There are many Delilahs and Jezebels with us today.

Young men and women need the starkness of this verse. The believer cannot assume that he or she might be able to exert influence on a prospective marriage partner that will lead to his or her salvation. We cannot go counter to God's law for marriage, presuming on His grace! There needs to be realistic cold thinking concerning mixed marriages.

Sometimes in our world things are far too fuzzy. We forget what a hard line there is between the child of God and the unbeliever. From the day a child enters kindergarten he needs to be reminded by his parents that he is *different*. Especially is this the case when it comes to marriage. If a person is 'kind,' or 'decent' we feel that a Christian could perhaps settle for this. We point to cases where after marriage the unbeliever has been won to Christ. Certainly Scripture encourages us to see that this can occur, but this is not God's law. Because He sometimes does reach down in His grace and save the unbelieving partner, we cannot presume upon Him to do this. We cannot spoil His image of Himself and the Church! We must marry only in the Lord. It is as clear as that!

We need to be much in prayer for our young people. Let us remind them of Solomon!

LIMITS OF SUBMISSION
Esther 1:10–21

God permitted His people to be carried away into captivity under an oriental monarch. Now He gives us a lesson from the life of the heathen queen of this monarch. What a surprising God!

Vashti took her life in her hands when she refused to allow herself to be used to gratify the lust of a roomful of drunken men. In her strong principle and her courage of conviction she is an example to the Christian woman who sometimes needs to be strengthened in this matter of the limits of submission.

God has made marriage and the home to be

the basic unit of society. He has ordained that its unity be preserved by alloting different functions or positions to each partner. The man has been endowed with special characteristics that are designed to suit him for leadership and protection. The woman has been endowed with special characteristics which suit her for following, helping, supporting. Though not so public a figure she is equally important as a partner in this unity.

With the fall of man came all sorts of distortions of this pattern. The man was not always the gentle, loving leader. Now he was often the tyrant, or sometimes the weak, ineffectual, easily-influenced non-leader. The woman was now likely to be a sullen or rebellious helper or else one who wanted to usurp leadership.

Redeemed man can and must have a redeemed marriage. In Christ marriage can be as God planned it in the beginning. This means that the woman must be submissive.

If the husband, however, is not a believer or is out of fellowship with his Lord there may come a time when the wife finds submission to him a denial of her own relationship to God. God must come first. If she is sure that submission on some point is displeasing to Him, then she must follow the example of Vashti of old and refuse to obey her husband.

If Vashti dared to defy her husband, surely a Christian woman should be courageous to render her first loyalty to her Saviour when a husband is demanding that she compromise her faith!

ANOTHER WOMAN'S COURAGE
Esther 4:10–17

We pay tribute to Vashti for setting limits to her submission to a heathen monarch. What do we say about the Jewish woman who succeeds her as favorite wife in the harem of this heathen monarch?

First we have to ask, What do we say about David and about others like him in earlier years? Nothing more harsh may be said about Esther than about them. Although she disobeyed God's creation mandate for marriage, she must not be singled out for a sin greater than that of David.

Having said this, let us turn to recognize the magnificent place in the history of her people that Esther filled. She, like Vashti, determined to go against the law in defiance of the king. She was forbidden by Persian law to approach him of her own accord. This was to risk death if he was not pleased at that moment to receive her. But she dared to do just this.

What a sense she and her cousin Mordecai had of the sovereignty of God! The line of the promised Messiah would not be broken off. Deliverance, as Mordecai reminded her, would come to the Jews from another quarter without her intervention. However, she dared to be used by God as He would grant.

How aware Esther was of her need of God's help! She was weak. She asked for fasting (with

the prayer that accompanied it) on the part of
'all the Jews' and of her own maidens. An ancient
'Day of Prayer'!

She did not have her eyes closed to the possibility that she might be put to death. But she was
willing, for the sake of her people and her God,
to proceed with this thing, undergirded by their
prayers. God rewarded her selflessness by preserving her life along with the life of her people.
Mordecai was right. The line of Messiah could
not be broken off. And God granted to Esther
the honor of being used to this end.

OUR CHILDREN'S SINS
Job 1:1–5

The Book of Job is a magnificent but strange
story. It is very moving. Verse 5 of chapter 1 is
the picture of a godly father who loves his children with a brave and honest love. We read,
'Early in the morning he would sacrifice a burnt
offering for each of them, thinking, "Perhaps my
children have sinned and cursed God in their
hearts" ' (1:5 NIV). Surely God heard the prayers of this great father-heart.

All through the lives of his children the Christian parent will be praying for them. Before birth
he will begin. Through their childhood he will
be praying that the Lord will grant them a new
heart. When they are professing Christians there
will be prayers for protection from sin, for guidance and direction, for strength and forgiveness.

The parent will pray for their vocational choices. He will pray for their marriages! Always, ever, he will pray for these children. When they are grown and no longer under his personal direction and care, still he will cast about them a mantle of protection as he prays. He will be like Job: 'Thus did Job continually' (1:5).

This is one of the facets of the covenant. In the covenant the child has the special protection and aura of the prayer of his parents! In the covenant the father's intercession is heard by the heavenly Father. The Covenant God is faithful. Are we?

JOB'S WIFE
Job 2:1–13

Job was sitting down among the ashes trying desperately to get relief from his discomfort by scraping with a piece of broken pottery the sore boils which covered him from the top of his head to the soles of his feet. His physical distress, coming so soon after the death of his children, was almost more than he could bear.

Who on earth could be expected to minister to a person with such a revolting physical appearance and malady? Who indeed but his wife? She should have been the one who would dress his sores. She should have been the one who would assure him of her continuing love, and of God's love.

But what does she do? She shows a complete

lack of understanding of his deep trouble. 'Dost thou still retain thine integrity?', she asks bitterly; 'Curse God and die' (2:9).

Job, hurt to the quick, rebukes her, 'Thou speakest as one of the foolish women speaketh. What? Shall we receive good at the hand of God, and shall we not receive evil?' In all his distress we read that Job 'did not sin with his lips' (2:10).

As wives and husbands, how understanding are we of the physical limitations and problems of our loved ones? And of the spiritual problems? We should 'sit where they sit' and try to understand their situation. Or, to use a familiar figure, we should try walking in their moccasins!

God wants the wife to be a helper and a support. He also wants the husband to 'give honour unto the wife, as unto the weaker vessel' (I Peter 3:7). Many of us have promised at marriage to take each other 'for better and for worse, in sickness and in health.' Do we really enter into the problems of our spouse?

HAPPINESS IN CORRECTION
Job 5:17–27

When sorrow or distress comes, what is our reaction? Do we recognize that it may be the chastening of the Lord? Do we look up to God and say, 'Thank you, God, for loving me enough to correct me when I need correction'?

Do our children realize that our correction of

them is something that should make them happy? Do they realize that it is an evidence of our love wanting to help them in their growth and development? Often they do and that is why children sometimes even ask for correction! They want to feel the security of a love that cares enough to correct. There is a real security in being in strong hands that know what they are doing.

But do our children realize that our correction of them can help them to understand the meaning of God's chastening? We should be helping them to see here again the parallel between the earthly and the heavenly that is evident all through God's Word, the one reminding us of the other and helping us to understand it.

And again we see the unity of Scripture and the unchangeable character of our God. We meet this same teaching concerning the chastening of the Lord again and again, and in a strikingly similar way centuries later in Hebrews 12:5–12. Our God does not change, nor do the needs of His creatures. The message of Job is for us and for our children.

MY GOD SINCE BIRTH
Psalm 22:1–10

David dispels the notion that there must be a dramatic experience of conversion to which a Christian can point as the beginning of his walk with God. God gave David faith when he was a babe in his mother's arms! In fact, the God who brought him from his mother's womb was his God from that time on.

Or before? David indicates that he existed as a person within the womb. God drew him out, a person on whom God's love was already fastened. 'From my mother's womb you have been my God' he says (22:10 NIV).

This is grace! This is the sovereignty of God in action in the realm of salvation. The teaching of sovereign grace did not originate with Paul! Here it is in the Book of Psalms many centuries before Paul.

How thankful we must be that our salvation is not something that depends upon us—our thoughts, our faith, our righteousness! It is all of Him. And sovereignly He reaches down, sometimes at birth, sometimes during youth, sometimes at the door of death. There is no pattern that we can discern. Sovereignly He acts. And how thankful we should be that He chose *us!*

WHEN MY FATHER AND MY MOTHER FORSAKE ME
Psalm 27

There is a story of an orphan who first came to understand the love of God when she was confronted with the comfort of verse 10: 'When my father and my mother forsake me, then the Lord will take me up' (27:10). Among men we can find no symbol of security more meaningful than that of parenthood. Parents are the ones to whom we go when all else fails.

But even parents can fail. In this world of sin and frailty parents can be less than the rock God planned them to be. And there are limits to the help they can provide. Man cannot hope to find any human being who can satisfy all his needs. A man is driven ultimately to God for the answer to his needs and the granting of the desires of his heart.

A child who can depend upon his parents has a security that will stand him in good stead. However, the Christian parent must never regard himself as God, the impregnable Rock. He must recognize his frailty. He must recognize that he, too, is a child. His greatest strength is God, not self. So the greatest favor he can grant his child is to point that child beyond himself to God.

David points us to God here. God, he is suggesting, is the *GREAT PARENT,* the prototype of human parents, the one who will not forsake His children.

WAITING
Psalm 40

David says he waited for God and God heard and established him, putting a new song in his mouth. This is a refrain we read often in Scripture and experience often in life. We pray. God does not answer immediately. He allows us to learn the lessons of trust. He allows us to learn lessons in persistent prayer. God makes us wait.

David expresses gratefulness to God in this Psalm. He has experienced God's faithfulness in the past and is emboldened to make more importunate requests. 'O Lord, make haste to help me' (40:13). 'Make no tarrying, O my God' (40:17). But God allowed him to wait and experience the strengthening of his faith before receiving his answer.

What a common trait is impatience! As parents we can have a lot to do with either nourishing or rooting out this weed in our children. The parent who regularly gives way to the compulsion to pick up baby at the first cry or to open the refrigerator at the first plea for a drink of milk is surely fostering impatience! The parent who follows a reasonable schedule in the household, a schedule which attempts to take into consideration the needs of all its members, is teaching the child to adapt himself to the world in which he will be living, and to discipline himself to wait!

This principle holds true particularly in regard to the gratification of physical desires. Is it unreasonable to consider the possibility that the child who has been used to having every physical desire met promptly, as a direct consequence may have to struggle the harder as a youth or adult with this same problem? Is it unreasonable to consider that this may apply also to sex? As parents we have a responsibility to help, not hinder, the development of self-control in our children.

When we teach our children to wait patiently for us and for others we are really giving them a lesson in self-control, in consideration for others and in waiting on the Lord! A difficult lesson this is to learn, but perhaps a more difficult one for us to teach! There is a plaque which reads, 'Lord, give me patience. And give it to me right now.' We smile at this because it speaks to us where we are.

WEDDING PSALM
Psalm 45

A Bible expositor when questioned concerning how many of the Psalms are Messianic replied that although he had not as yet made an exhaustive study he was of the opinion that 150 of them are! Even we who are lesser authorities can quickly see that Psalm 45 is describing our heavenly Bridegroom!

'Thy throne, O God, is for ever and ever' (45:6). This is the King who is described here. And of what other King could it be said, 'He is thy Lord; and worship thou him' (45:11).

This Psalm is talking about us then! We are the queen-bride. Whatever the immediate reference, the ultimate prophetic reference is to the church. But what beauty do we have that the King will greatly desire? We have only the beauty He gives us, the beauty of holiness wrought by His own indwelling Spirit.

We can and must adorn ourselves to fit our

station, an adorning of a meek spirit. A humble submission to the Husband is fitting for us. Never can we be satisfied that we are really worthy to be the Bride of such an One!

At the same time we can rest in His acceptance. 'For when we were yet without strength, in due time Christ died for the ungodly' (Romans 5:6). He accepted us as we were and then began to make us what he wants us to be!

This is *our* wedding Psalm.

GUILT
Psalm 51

David says to his God, 'Against thee, thee only, have I sinned, and done this evil in thy sight' (51:4). Sin is not only manward, it is Godward! God identifies Himself with His people. Sin against God's people is sin against God Himself.

However, even sin against unbelievers is sin against God, because God has told us to be holy. He desires our sanctification, He requires obedience to His law. So no matter whom we wrong, we sin against God and are guilty before Him.

When as parents we sin against each other or against our children we need to acknowledge this sin. We need to ask forgiveness of the offended one. But we need to go further and ask forgiveness of God Himself.

Guilt is blamed for all sorts of ill-effects upon the mind and personality. We read of persons who all their lives have been tortured by guilt feelings over a deed committed in youth, a deed which may or may not have been serious and may or may not have been really the fault of the person in question. So guilt is sometimes represented as being bad, something to be avoided.

But we need not be afraid of true guilt which springs from a knowledge of the holiness of God and His law. This guilt may and should issue in repentance as a man confesses his sin and comes to God through Christ. Guilt thus brought to God will be buried in the depths of the sea, along with the sin which occasioned it. A true sense of guilt is really the first step toward the liberation of the spirit!

The nature of guilt and the handling of guilt are two of the most significant lessons we have to teach our children. And all we need to know about this is in God's Word. Psalm 51 is an excellent place to begin to understand these truths and the way God graciously enables us to handle them.

PERPETUAL CHAIN
Psalm 78:1–22

We could go on to read this entire chapter. The whole Psalm is a powerfully drawn picture of God's goodness to His people, their turning from Him in unbelief, their punishment and return. It is a story God wants us to remember and profit from.

Many of us have heard this story from our fathers in the faith and often from our fathers in the flesh. It is not to rest with us. We are not to hide it from our children. It is to be handed down from generation to generation 'that they might set their hope in God and not forget the works of God, but keep his commandments' (78:7).

This is the picture of the perpetual chain of belief. It is a beautiful picture in which we have a wonderful part, but one that would really frighten us were it not for our faith in God's love and power. Nothing must cause us to let the chain break with us—no lack of knowledge of God's Word, no supposed inability to communicate it, no reluctance to oppose our children, no fear of rebuff. It is *God* who has established this plan and program. It is to Him we are responsible!

It is also God who will prosper our testimony. Ultimately it is God who will be using us as His link in this golden chain of belief. He will not leave Himself without a testimony.

HOME BEHAVIOR
Psalm 101

You have heard, perhaps, the story of a certain man who claimed to be sinless. An acquaintance once made the comment to him, 'I'd like to talk to your wife about that.' Immediately the man flew into a rage.

It is in the home where we let down the bars. It may be possible to keep a fairly consistent outward front as we go among our associates in the office, at the market, at church. The constant friction of assorted personalities in the home day after day is what brings out the sinful nature that still lurks within even the one who may have proceeded quite far along the road of sanctification!

David in this Psalm is talking about his home. He says, 'I will walk within my house in the integrity of my heart' (101:2 NASB). David's house was the palace. In it lived many servants and the royal entourage as well as his family. We may be sure he had the same temptation there as we do in our home to let down the bars and give in to the weakness of the flesh. However, notice how the entire Psalm is a declaration of his intent to glorify God in his house. He wants no deceit, lying, pride, gossiping. He will choose those to live in his house from among people who purpose to keep God's laws. He will search them out and bring them to live there. Those who would spoil the atmosphere of peace in the house will not be permitted to remain!

David surely has a lesson for us. O Lord, help us by Your Spirit to keep David's resolve: 'I will walk within my house in the integrity of my heart.'

CLEANSING
Psalm 119:9–16

The story is told of an elderly lady who went to her minister, troubled. 'I read the Bible,' she told him, 'but I cannot seem to remember what I read.'

The wise minister told her to fill a sieve with water. This discouraging task proved not at all helpful to her case. 'But,' said the minister, 'see how clean the sieve is!' We may not remember all we read, but it cleanses us.

Not only the young man of Psalm 119:9, but the older person, too, needs the method for cleansing set forth here. Verse 11 spells it out. All of us need to hide God's Word in our heart that we might not sin against Him—that we might be cleansed. Verse 9 says: 'How can a young man keep his way pure?' (NIV) This is not only for initial cleansing but for daily cleansing, too.

What does it mean to hide God's Word in our hearts? This hiding, or 'treasuring,' has many aspects. We need to understand Bible history, the contents of the books, the system of doctrine, the practical injunctions for living. In a day when memorization is considered outmoded, we must not forget to memorize God's Word and help our children to memorize it, too. How many saints of God have borne testimony to the peace and strength they have found at times of great stress or persecution in the Word of God treasured in their hearts! Not only in extreme situations, but every day we need to have the words of God at the tip of our tongue.

Cleansing of the ways is essential for all ages. God's Word is our spiritual detergent!

THE COMPLETE MARRIAGE
Psalm 127

In one sense a marriage is complete when God is at its center. God made man and woman the same in essence but with different gifts. They were to complement or complete each other and together form a social unity. By nature each of us has a God-shaped vacuum within. Unfortunately some persons marry in order to have this filled, but then find that the marriage partner is not able to fill it. The fact is, each one has a vacuum of his own! In marriage, then, there is just one larger, combined space! In the complete marriage God Himself fills it.

There is another sense in which we speak of completeness in marriage. In order that a marriage may be conformed to God's perfect design there will ordinarily be progeny. 'Children are an heritage of the Lord' (127:3). Made in the image of God, man is creative. God enables him to be an instrument in the bringing forth of a completely new human being! In fact he even commanded 'male and female' to 'be fruitful and multiply and replenish the earth' (Genesis 1:28).

[117]

There are men and women today who for selfish reasons do not want to be tied down to marriage and to a home. They want to be free to make an impact upon the world and to do something really big and creative. Or they want to be free just to indulge themselves. These people include the women who scorn what they would call the prosaic humdrum of home life which they say does not challenge their capabilities. They are turning their backs upon the fulfilment that God grants in a marriage which is complete, with God in the center and with children as the heritage.

HOME—HEAVEN
Psalm 128

Blessing (happiness from God) comes from fearing God and walking in His love. The picture of blessing in this Psalm is a home complete with wife and children.

Man was made by God to be a social being. Not only was he made to enjoy being with people, he was made to enjoy being with his own people, the same people, day after day and year after year in the same place, home. Man was made to flourish in the environment of a family. This family needs a base. Man needs a place to which he can return and find love, a place where he belongs.

A haunting contemporary song speaks of 'all

the lonely people.' Our world today is filled with lonely people. Many of these are people who have left their homes to find something they thought would be better. Ironically, that which they have turned their backs upon is that which they need and which needs them.

There can be no emptiness, meaninglessness, alienation when we are part of a family which fears the Lord and is walking in His way. According to the Master Planner the needs of men are to be met in the home. When He is present, our spiritual needs are met there, too.

God wanted us to know something of what heaven will be, so He planned for us homes, Christian homes.

FAMILY SOLIDARITY
Psalms 133 and 134

Solidarity or unity is a beautiful thing in the family of God. Through love and the exercise of our gifts we grow as a church into a real unity in Christ. The church needs to become increasingly more aware of this.

And here again, the church, the family of God, is reflected or pictured in the human, biological family. There need be no alienation or generation gap if each member is in God's family, too.

How sad is disunity in the family. Are there in your home any who mar the goodness and pleasantness by the very fact that they are not children of God? Between believers and unbelievers is a barrier, a real barrier that may not be seen with the physical eye, yet may be felt by the sensitive soul. It is possible for this barrier to exist anywhere in the family; on one side, believers, on the other side, unbelievers.

But this barrier is not insurmountable. Were we to draw a family tree we should sketch this barrier with a dotted line because it is a barrier which may be broken down by God's grace! Those who are on the Lord's side must be instant in prayer to Him that this may be the case. The daily prayer must be that the family may be unified in Christ!

CORRECTION OUT OF LOVE
Proverbs 3:1-12

'My son, despise not the chastening of the Lord' (3:11). We have seen this in Job. We shall read it again later. Maybe we should just skip over it here.

But so full is our life of illness, disappointment, frustration, even persecution, that we need to be reminded often and vigorously that these things are used for our growth in the Lord. We need to be reminded often that no matter how bad things seem to be, the Lord is at the helm, and He is working out in our lives things that will be to His glory and for our good. He is often correcting us out of love.

Especially in our day we need to be reminded

to train our children in accordance with this pattern that God has set forth in His relationship with us. Conversely, as we correct our children in love we are setting forth the relationship between God and His children!

There is no room for the vengeful, tyrannical, emotional, spiteful correction of children. Nor is there room for the resentful, sulky, self-pitying child. This applies in our own homes, but it applies as well in the church, the household of God.

Correction is one of the means God uses for causing us to grow in grace. Our parents, the leaders in our churches, our elders in the faith, are to encourage us in our sanctification. We in turn are to aid others, including our own children.

GET WISDOM
Proverbs 4:1–13

Solomon pays real tribute to David his father who truly loved him and taught him to seek wisdom. We can glean from this picture something which would contribute toward Solomon's choosing from God the gift of wisdom for himself.

Now Solomon is passing this advice on to his children. 'Get wisdom. Get understanding' (4:5). What does he mean by wisdom? Certainly this is not a mere worldly wisdom. With this section we must compare chapter 1, verse 7, and other verses like it: 'The fear of the Lord is the beginning of knowledge.' This is a wisdom which is based upon an understanding of God the Creator-

Sustainer-Redeemer. This is what we are to strive for and to enjoin our children to strive for.

In all our education as people of God we work from the presupposition of the existence of God, the God who reveals Himself in Scripture. We cannot have true knowledge or the wisdom to utilize it unless we begin with God.

This orientation is a major element in the genius of the Christian School. If children are in such an educational system and atmosphere they will be learning by the power of the Spirit of God that the fear of the Lord is the basis of all true thinking.

If our children are not in this kind of a school, what an added responsibility we have! Our efforts at home and in the church have to be even more assiduously geared toward the undergirding of the child for the task of approaching with Christian presuppositions all the subject matter of the classroom and of the world at large. He needs to be shown how to weigh, consider and analyze whatever he meets and be able to see the fallacies resulting from beginning with another premise.

'Take fast hold of instruction; let her not go: keep her; for she is thy life!' (4:13)

SEX EDUCATION
Proverbs 5:15–23

We probably do not regard the Bible as a manual on sex education, but it is! When it has been taken seriously its effects have been significant and far-reaching.

The Proverbs show an openness in speaking about sex which has not always existed through history. In Old Testament times wealthier men sometimes had several wives. Because of the hardness of their hearts God even permitted divorce, but men *knew* what was right. They understood that God made marriage to be an exclusive, lifelong relationship. The harlot was frowned upon. Infidelity to their God on the part of His people was compared to the unfaithfulness of a marriage partner. These things are freely discussed in God's holy Book.

Sex within marriage was accepted as good and honorable. This is evident in today's reading and it is expressed even more fully in the Song of Solomon. One would be blind not to see in Scripture that we have been given sex to enjoy in its God-appointed context.

In the girl's dormitory of a certain college there was posted a cartoon of a young boy, books in hand, evidently just returned home after school and standing inside his front door. He announces, 'OK, everyone in this house, please stand advised that I, Thomas P. Thompson, have this day made a complete fool of myself in Sex Education class by repeating elaborate stories concerning storks told me by certain parties residing herein.'

If misinformation or lack of information concerning sex causes embarrassment to our children, that is a small thing compared to the way in which it can so affect their attitudes and emotions that a wholesome, healthy sex life within their marriage may be difficult to achieve. Christian parents cannot shield their children from the torrents of ugly and distorted sex information and mis-information that is emptied upon them from every side. They *can* implant the attitudes toward sex which the Bible offers. Failure to do this is failure to educate them fully in God's truth.

A VEGETARIAN MEAL
Proverbs 15:1–17

Who would choose a vegetable platter if filet mignon or lobster were to be had? Rather, if the vegetables were served up with love and the meat with hate, who would hesitate to choose the meatless meal? In men's blindness this truth is often forgotten.

This is no wonder because it is difficult to love. When there is deceit, rebellion, nastiness in the family, how can the parent still love? How can a total atmosphere of love be maintained when even one family member gets out of line? How can you listen, listen, listen and forgive, forgive, forgive? It is very difficult to love.

Compared to loving it is easy to serve a steak dinner, to buy tape decks and color television. Because there are easier things to provide for the family parents often consider them as substitutes for love. They are regarded as vehicles for demonstrating love. Material gifts MAY display love, but only if they are given IN LOVE and only if love is also displayed in other ways.

One of the most difficult ways to demonstrate love is to maintain discipline in accordance with God's law. To do this in the home may even be the most God-like way in which we may express our love.

Some Christian families have the custom of holding hands around the table during the thanksgiving at meals. This is a beautiful symbol of a home where love is and a mute testimony to the children and to guests, even if a meatless meal is being served!

COMMUNICATION
Proverbs 18:1–13

Sometimes we act as though communication is something that has only recently been discovered! Communication is said to be the great need in personal relationships. There is a stress upon the need to listen, to find out what makes the other person tick. We are urged really to get to know one another, and to be willing to express our own needs to others through our words and our actions.

It is surely true that this is a great need. It is surely true that a lack of adequate communication causes many of our interpersonal problems.

However, the value of good communication is not something that has *recently* been discovered!

[125]

All the Scriptures stress it. We saw it in Genesis. Now we see it in the Book of Proverbs. In this brief section alone note the emphasis upon proper and adequate communication.

A foolish person does not want to understand. He only wants to speak his own mind. He fails to listen because he is too busy talking about his own concerns or thinking what he is to say next! He says things that stir up anger. His tongue causes much trouble. In fact, it brings about his own destruction. The words of a whisperer are taken in and stored away deep inside men's minds and consciences. It is folly to give an answer before one hears!

In training children, the use of the Book of Proverbs is highly beneficial. It is dangerous for the parent to present his own ideas as truth. To be able to point to objective truth, God's truth, and to teach God's very words is wonderful. How helpful it is for a child to grow up with the Proverbs in his heart! Much trouble would be avoided if men learned this wisdom: 'He that answereth a matter before he heareth it, it is folly and shame unto him' (18:13), or 'A fool does not delight in understanding, but only in revealing his own mind' (18:2 NASB).

SPIRITS, WIVES AND FRIENDS
Proverbs 18:14–24

Spirits! The spirit of man is tough but tender. It carries him through times of illness. It sustains him during difficult seasons. On the other hand, it can easily be bruised. A brother who is offended is alienated. If a man's spirit is wounded he is a broken man. The wisdom and understanding of the Lord cause us to recognize our need to respect others and to treat them with dignity. We need as parents especially to pray that God will help us not to wound the spirit of a child! We must be alert, for example, to the degree of awareness a child has to the casual comments which, although not even directed to him, find their way into his inner consciousness and rankle and wound.

Wives! God gave man a great favor when He made woman to be his helper. This is true in a general way for all mankind, because marriage is given to all for the orderly managing of society. God, in His common grace, has granted much joy to men through marriage. How special, though, is the Christian wife who seeks for her husband good and not ill all his days. Men, never take for granted this favor God has given you!

Friends! Friends, too, are a blessing from God. Friendships are reciprocal. Each man reaches out and the hands touch. A relationship that grows up from mutual interests and ideals and purposes can be a relationship that is even closer than some family relationships where there are differences of belief and interests. Abraham was called a friend of God (James 2:23). And Jesus told His disciples that they were His friends (John 15:15).

Spirits, wives and friends! These verses seem to deal with different subjects, but they are all concerned with interpersonal relationships. How good God is not only to give us people in our lives to assuage the loneliness of the human heart, but also to give us directions for improving the relationships we sustain with them!

WHILE THERE IS HOPE
Proverbs 19:9–23

'While there is hope!' we read in verse 18. This striking phrase carries with it the intimation that the day will come when there is not going to be any hope. What does God mean by this?

He may mean that death will come to all. After death there is no hope of changing one's standing with God. There is no so-called second chance.

He may mean that the day will come when the child will be beyond the control and influence of the home. The years of training will be over and the child will be on his own.

But it is likely that God here is expressing in another way what He declares so fearfully in Romans 1. As a person repeatedly refuses the wooings of the Holy Spirit, the overtures of the love of God, he is more and more confirmed in his sinful way. Progressively God gives him up to go his own way and to live his own life. He is increasingly more confirmed in his sinful walk and settled in unbelief.

So important is this chastening, in the light of the phrase 'while there is hope,' that the parent is not to let his soul be swayed by tears from his purposeful training. Here we come to a delicate point. It *is* difficult to see your beloved child cry. And it takes a firm hand to persist in training when the son or daughter reacts with tears.

One of the complicating factors is the way the child, even in infancy, learns to use tears as a weapon. One woman we know well remembers clearly from the early teen years forcing the tears out in order to sway her parents. In the face of this it behoves us to give our principles of training a hard look in the light of God's Word and then prayerfully, gently proceed with our discipline.

All stems back to our sinful nature. 'There are many devices in a man's heart' (19:21).

God lets us cry, doesn't He? Don't we have to acknowledge the place sorrow has had in the making of what we are?

IN THE WAY HE SHOULD GO
Proverbs 22:1–16

Verse 6 is a comforting promise to parents. In periods of a child's growing up, with the rebellion that sometimes accompanies it, this verse has been quoted with a heart full of trust in the Lord and with a faith that He will answer prayers for the salvation of covenant children.

Sometimes it has been quoted too glibly by parents who have not, in fact, been as faithful as the verse would require in training their children. Who among us has been completely faithful? We must be on guard against quoting this verse presumptuously.

Let us look at the verse more carefully. The word translated *train up* means in the Hebrew *initiate* or *dedicate*. The Hebrew word for *catechise* is drawn from this word, too. The child is to be initiated into the things of the Lord, dedicated as a temple of the Holy Spirit, catechised in the truth. The phrase *in his way* has the meaning of *in the mouth of his way* in the Hebrew, or *at the beginning of his way*.

The Proverb is saying that we should at the earliest possible time introduce the child to God's truth, carefully teaching him God's Word. If we do this he will not depart from the way of the Lord as he grows into adult years. There may be a period of time before he accepts these truths for himself. But the time of blessing will come.

This verse is a proverb, a statement of the way things generally are. We might say, 'The apple does not fall far from the tree'; or 'Like father, like son.' These are proverbs, too, and say something very similar. We recognize that they do not always apply. They picture the normal course or sequence of events.

The mistake comes when this verse is used as a blanket promise by God that without fail every child trained in the faith will become a Christian. This is contrary to other portions of Scripture. Our covenant God is sovereign in salvation and He normally works in families, rewarding believing parents with believing children. Scripture does not teach that *every* child of the covenant will confess Him. There are those who, despite the influences and training of a godly home, have consistently and permanently refused to bow the knee to the God of their fathers.

This verse *is* a comfort. But most of all it is a spur to the parent to train his child in God's way, heeding the directions of verse 15: 'Foolishness is bound in the heart of a child; but the rod of correction shall drive it far from him.'

RADICAL MEANS
Proverbs 23:12–26

Physical punishment is considered by many parents to be obsolete and cruel, the venting of parental wrath. It is equated with child-beating and it would even be considered by some an infringement upon the child's 'rights.' Its mention in Scripture in this passage and others is embarrassing to some Christians. But we must not suppose ourselves to be more *humane* than God. He knows the power of sin and the perverseness of fallen man better than we do. Punishment, whether physical or not, must be effective. That is the force of this verse.

Verses 13 and 14 acknowledge that the sin of man is so insidious that it cannot be dealt with except by the use of radical means. And by 'radical' we stress that the means must go to the root. Mowing the lawn will not destroy weeds permanently! The dandelions that infest it must be rooted out completely. Children differ greatly. A gentle reproof is not always sufficient to impress upon some the seriousness of wrong behavior. Isolation, deprivation, or as a last resort physical punishment have to be employed with some children to underscore the necessity of obedience.

A young girl said, 'I wish I had been spanked. I was beaten, but not spanked.' Correction *in love* under God is not cruel. It is life-giving. It will not harm the child. It will only benefit him by pointing out God's intense hatred for sin and our need to conform to His law. 'The rod and reproof give wisdom,' we read in Proverbs 29:15, 'but a child left to himself bringeth his mother to shame.'

Gilbert and Sullivan have a ditty, 'Let the punishment fit the crime.' This is a good rule for the home on occasions. When the offense warrants it the Christian parent need not feel guilty for using physical punishment in a calm, purposeful manner, out of love for the child and for the God who has placed this child under his care with directions for his nurture. Indeed, such a parent should feel guilty when he does *not* obey God in this respect!

And always must the forgiving spirit of the earthly father and heavenly Father be made apparent along with the punishment.

THE VIRTUOUS WOMAN
Proverbs 31:10–31

Christianity is blamed by some people today for the degradation of women. They point to isolated verses which they claim teach that the woman is to be slavishly submissive and they declare that from this teaching male chauvinism developed.

It is possible that a superficial reading of the Scriptures by a sin-darkened intellect could result in a distorted view of what submission means and what the Biblical picture of the woman is. In actual fact, it is the fall of man with its ensuing sin that is responsible for male chauvinism. Surely Proverbs 31 does not picture a degraded woman, crushed under the domination of her husband and barred from challenging avenues of endeavor and from liberties that are hers under God.

Proverbs 31 is a picture of a *complete* woman, one who recognizes what her chief fulfilment is and who delights in it. She is a woman who knows who and what she is, glad that she is a woman and glad to occupy her own special sphere of influence!

The virtuous woman of this chapter is a hard worker. She applies herself assiduously and faithfully to her tasks. These tasks are tedious and time-consuming. She does not have an electric kitchen. The materials she has to work with do not have the variety that ours have. But she is not bored or idle. She works willingly and joyfully. What is the secret?

Basically, the secret is her motivation, to serve the Lord and honor Him. Another important ingredient in all this is tucked away in verse 28: her husband appreciates her! He praises her. She is very special to him and he wants her and others to know it.

A husband like that *helps* a woman to be 'virtuous.' That's just the way women are!

REMEMBER YOUR CREATOR
Ecclesiastes 12

Are you young? The Preacher would have you remember your Creator now. Be advised that God wants your *whole* life. He wants the vigor of your youth! He is not a toy that you can play with and push aside until you are just too bored with everything else and finally feel like condescending to heed Him. The longer you put off making a commitment to Him the more difficult it will be to kneel and bow your head. As previously mentioned, another Preacher, Paul, warned the Romans centuries after Solomon, that when we sink more and more into our sinful unbelief God may give us up more and more. Remember your Creator now!

Are you older? Are these evil days for you? Old age is presented here as vanity. Here we see old age as weakened vitality, loss of the faculties, the palsied limb, the toothless mouth, the dim eyes and unhearing ears, the fear of heights, the fear of everything! Graphically the preacher-poet presents it, and this is old age as mankind generally has had to face it since the fall. It is emptiness.

If, however, in the providence of God we do remember Him in our youth, old age with all its infirmities can be more beautiful than the preacher points out here. It can be the old age of still another preacher, the apostle John, whose heart of love still reached to his children in the faith and whose heart rejoiced to see them walk in the truth! When our walk with God has been maintained through the years, old age is a time of peace and hope which transcends physical limitations and reaches out towards eternity.

> Grow old along with me!
> The best is yet to be,
> The last of life, for which the
>   first was made:
> Our times are in His hand
> Who saith, 'A whole I planned,
> Youth shows but half, trust God:
>   see all, nor be afraid!'*

*Browning, Robert. *Rabbi Ben Ezra* (Stanza I).

THE SONG OF SONGS
Song of Solomon 1

The Bible is the Book of books. Christ is the King of kings. This poem is the Song of songs! This is the language of superlatives.

Yet this book was in the early Christian era an embarrassment for both the rabbis and the Christian divines. Probably influenced by notions that associated the body with sin, they were apologetic for its openness in handling the romantic theme and the physical aspects of love. Out of their position they were forced to support Scripture. This book, however, strained their orthodoxy. So in their dilemma they invented fanciful explanations for the Song, according to which the references were said to allude exclusively to the relationship between Christ and the church. In fact, the Authorized Version inserts this interpretation into the chapter headings, which are not part of the original text. We can presume that these chapter headings have been through the years in a large measure responsible for the persistence of this extreme interpretation.

And indeed this purely allegorical interpretation does persist. One of the current commentators compares the two breasts mentioned in chapter 1:13 to the Old and New Testaments and he compares the 'bundle of myrrh' lying between them to Christ. If you picked up this book without previous bias, would you think of this figure in that light? Does this explanation satisfy you? Does God wish to establish an élite who alone can interpret Scripture to the masses? There are doubtless difficulties in understanding this book, partly because it is not always clear who is speaking. But as you read this chapter, is it not evident that God is saying that sex is good and that manifestations of romantic love are good and acceptable between those who are entitled to them?

God made man and woman to desire each other and enjoy each other physically. We do not apologize for the presence in the Bible of a book which plainly indicates this! Rather we may be glad that He saw fit to reveal to us His approbation of romantic love.

We will read this entire book together. Let us struggle to see what God is saying here for us today, for this husband and this wife!

HIS BANNER . . . WAS LOVE
Song of Solomon 2

After what was said yesterday we must hasten to make a clarifying comment. We have seen throughout Scripture that God uses imagery to reveal His truth and that one of His favorite images is marriage. Old and New Testament alike speak of God as the husband and His people as the wife. When His people are unfaithful God rebukes them for going a-whoring after strange gods and playing the harlot. We are all familiar with Paul's striking words concerning Christ and the church placed parallel to his comments concerning the husband and wife. In Revelation John tells us that there will one day be the marriage supper of the Lamb!

When we are objecting to the fanciful interpretation of the Song of Solomon we are not denying this parallel between the earthly marriage and the heavenly marriage. It is a very precious experience to contemplate the love between the Saviour and His Bride while we read this poem.

In Scripture we must note, however, that there are often two applications: first, the immediate one, and second, the spiritual or prophetic one. The problem with a *purely* allegorical interpretation is that the immediate application is lost. This song is, immediately, a love song. It is an idyllic picture of the man-woman relationship. What it shows in the immediate sense is the progress of love and its delights. While it is oriental in style, it is timeless and we can look at it today without any embarrassment which must hastily be covered up with detailed allegory.

The second or prophetic and spiritual application of this book certainly points forward to the relationship between Christ and the church His beloved. As we read we can contemplate the ineffable delight in the presence of the loved one. We marvel at the love of God for us. We find in exquisite expression the love we have for Him—its longing, its intensity, its certainty, its joy!

Indeed, 'His banner over me was love' (2:4b).

In our marriage we experience just enough of what this means to help us understand its higher application! Thank You, God.

WHOM MY SOUL LOVETH
Song of Solomon 3

As a hangover from an earlier day there are Christian couples even now who enter marriage with a guilt feeling about sex. They cannot rid themselves of the notion that somehow sex is dirty or shameful. This is an attitude from which the Lord wants the Christian to be liberated.

God made the body of the woman with every line and proportion and curve and texture. He made man to delight in each characteristic. This He did to prove a source of delight in marriage. He did it, too, as part of His plan for His creatures to reproduce after their kind. It is not sinful for husband and wife to enjoy each other in a physical way as well as a spiritual way. It is perfectly appropriate for the act of marriage to follow devotions. Sex is a real nourishment for our whole being. Nor is it a sin for us to enjoy the fact that we enjoy one another! God made it to be this way.

The husband and wife should be able to communicate freely to each other any problems in sexual adjustment. We should feel free to pray that God would enable us to enjoy this means of expressing love in a way that is more complete.

If it appears necessary, we should not hesitate to seek advice from qualified persons.

The *one flesh* concept of marriage cannot thrive when the flesh is cheating the flesh, or bristling against the flesh, or tensing up against the flesh. There needs to be in marriage a relaxed peacefulness of conscience and a liberation of emotion if God's plan for the man and woman is to be realized!

THOU ART FAIR, MY LOVE
Song of Solomon 4

When we speak of openness in communication about sex we are not speaking of boldness, crudeness, ugliness. In the Song of Solomon we do not find pornography. There is delicacy and restraint.

Nor are we speaking of public display or profession of affection. There is nothing of the theatrical. There is something very intimate about this Song. Lovers thrive on being alone together. This, we can note, is one of the principles that points to the relationship between our Heavenly Bridegroom and His bride; the believer enjoys fellowship with his Saviour away from the world.

We are not speaking, either, as we talk about openness, of the bawdiness, the ugly humor that so often characterizes secular literature and the stage and screen. Sex is not in this Song an object for joking. The delight in sex may have a lightness at times, but the lightness is that of joy and liberty and confidence. It is not the lightness of a thoughtless surface relationship.

Nor is this purely physical communication. The sex act itself is only a part of the whole relationship. Husband and wife are not two animals. They are two human beings, two whole persons, enjoying a total union. They are enjoying a union of body, yes, but a union also of mind and of spirit.

In beautiful poetic imagery the chapter closes with an invitation: 'Let my beloved come to his garden, and eat of its choicest fruits.' The relationship has deepened. We have reached in our Song the threshold of marriage, the consummation of the love which has been growing.

The man and the woman who are in Christ Jesus can and should appropriate the words, the attitudes, the experience of the Shulamite maiden and her Shepherd King Lover. Else why has God given us this book? He does not tease and deceive His children!

ALTOGETHER LOVELY
Song of Solomon 5

'What is thy beloved more than another beloved?' (5:9) A beautiful thought lies in this question! How is it that a man regards one woman as so special above others, and she him?

Often we see a rather homely girl who is the beloved of a fine-looking man. 'What does he see in her?' we ask. He does see something very special in her that we do not see, because it is true that *love sees*. Love is not blind, it sees!

As we grow older we become aware when we look in the mirror that our physical beauty is fading along with our youth, but still our lover sees in us loveliness! The beauty is partly in *his* eye and *his* heart. What he sees is all tied up with the youth that was there, and with the kind heart and the loving deeds that characterize his beloved one. 'Beauty is in the eye of the beholder.'*

The world cannot understand our love for our Saviour. Why those hours in church? Why those dollars in the offering? Why that joy in fellowship with His children? Why a life 'wasted' on the mission field? 'What is your beloved more than another beloved?'

The world cannot understand, either—and here we join in the wonderment—how the Heavenly Bridegroom can love us! We fail Him. We grieve Him. We disobey. Yet He loves!

And is it not a beautiful thing how a man responds to such love as the Saviour's? The acceptance and peace and joy that flourish in a heart which knows the love of Christ will transform the unlovely. 'The desert shall rejoice, and blossom as the rose' (Isaiah 35:1).

Lord Jesus, You are 'altogether lovely.' Increase our love for You and our love for one another.

* Hungerford, Margaret W. *Molly Bawn*, chap. 12.

I AM MY BELOVED'S AND MY BELOVED IS MINE
Song of Solomon 6

A woman rightly resents being considered a sex object. As we have said, there are some who claim that this concept of woman stems from the Scriptures. This is a gross perversion. What help does this Song give us in understanding God's design for the woman?

It is interesting to note that in this poem there is a reciprocal enjoyment. The Shepherd King Lover expresses his appreciation for the beauty of his beloved here in verses 4–10. The Shulamite does likewise for him in chapter 5:10–16. This is a relationship of mutual loving and being loved.

Through the years the place of woman has changed, now for better, now for worse. How can people today expect us to believe that woman is experiencing a real improvement in her lot? The Playboy philosophy is with us and our world needs to see over against that the pure beauty of the Song of songs. Here is a woman who stands tall beside her man. They are equals. They are both thinking, feeling persons who desire each other and experience a mutual enjoyment of each other. There is no exploitation. There is liberty!

Does the world see in us, whether we are newlyweds or grandparents, the plan of God for marriage? Are we experiencing a redeemed relationship? If we are, we are being an unconscious testimony to a sick and dying world of what life is at its best!

HIS DESIRE IS TOWARD ME
Song of Solomon 7

Perhaps we shall not be sexually compatible, the young couple worries. Perhaps we should experiment and find out in advance to avoid incompatibility after marriage. This is the thesis for trial marriage.

What a pity that men and women are so misled! In this kind of relationship how can the true confidence of total permanent giving be experienced? Here is the relationship of this Song: 'I am my beloved's; and he is mine' (6:3). Not just tonight! Not until we decide it won't work! Not until he leaves for someone else! Till death!

The totality of this confidence is not only in duration. It is in the whole life experience. There is no trial period to see whether there is sexual compatibility. There is complete commitment that is willing to work on problems that may exist until they yield. It is a relationship that embraces everything around the clock. It is his kiss at the door. The holding of hands during prayer. The smile in the eyes across a crowded room. There is a constant reassurance of a belonging to each other.

The marriage where God is, the marriage for life, has, too, the confidence that tomorrow will bring an even closer relationship. There is no fear that it will not last. Rather, there is an assurance that as God does His work of sanctification in husband and wife they will be better able to know the meaning of selfless love. In a very real sense we may say that sanctification is the hope of Christian marriage.

'His desire is toward me' (7:10). Beautiful words of confidence with respect to the human lover! Amazing words of confidence with respect to the heavenly Bridegroom!

THE FLAME OF THE LORD
Song of Solomon 8

Today the word *love* is frequently a synonym for lust or infatuation. It can call to mind illicit relationships outside marriage as well as selfishness, jealousy and cruelty within marriage. Living in the midst of a fallen people we find it difficult to conceive of love as being a 'flame of Jehovah' (8:6 NASB).

The figure of fire in this passage pictures an open hearth where a controlled flame with fascinating colors and ever-changing form climbs and reaches out, enveloping the whole log. This is love in the high sense experienced by the husband and wife under God. This is God's gift to the husband and wife—'the flame of Jehovah.'

The apostle Paul uses this same figure of fire for lust. 'It is better,' he says, 'to marry than to burn' (1 Corinthians 7:9b). Here our minds conjure up a fire out of control which destroys and consumes, leaving ugly ashes in its trail.

The Song of Solomon may remind us of the time before the fall, when love was altogether pure and holy, not lustful. Adam and Eve were naked and they were not ashamed. There was no sin.

The Song of Solomon shows us the relationship which can and should obtain in the redeemed marriage. The new creature in Christ is renewed in his love life as well as in other aspects of his life. He is enabled more and more to experience the beauty and purity of love and to express it tenderly and selflessly.

Thank You, God, for the gift of romantic love. Thank You that it is a flame You have sent, a flame that cannot be quenched by many waters or drowned by floods. And thank You more than that for Your own love to us which makes the strongest of human loves appear a mere shadowy flicker!

REBELLIOUS CHILDREN
Isaiah 1:1–9

In the Song of Solomon we have a poem of love on the human and on the divine level. It is a beautiful pastoral symphony.

In Isaiah we have an abrupt change. The beauty of language and thought rubs shoulders with the

[146]

starkness and ugliness of sin. Right here in the second verse we see pictured a home whose spiritual climate is fraught with rebellion!

Are we parents surprised when our children are rebellious? Let us read this verse: 'I have nourished and brought up children, and they have rebelled against me!' says the Lord God (1:2). Can it be said that God is not the perfect Father? If His children turned from Him and His truth, why should it be so surprising that sometimes the children of imperfect human fathers are prodigal?

Parents who have prayerfully sought to train their children for the Lord must not condemn themselves unmercifully if they are greeted by rebellion. They must examine themselves, and ask the forgiveness of God as they discover areas where they have failed. They must continue to pray and wait the Lord's time for their children's return. In the end they must kneel to His providence in adoration and love.

We cannot possibly see what God is doing. How often a period of youthful rebellion and waywardness is turned by the Lord to blessing! Sometimes it is blessing to the parent as he learns new truths about himself and God's way. Often it is a blessing to the young person involved as he experiences God's forgiveness. Many times it is a blessing to other people as they observe a transformed life which can be nothing but the work of God's Spirit!

But let not parents whose children do not experience an open, dramatic period of rebellion, glory in their own abilities in child-rearing or their own piety. They may not say, 'See how our children have turned out. That is what comes from obeying God in the home.' These parents, too, must bow before the Sovereign God and humbly thank Him for His grace!

LINE UPON LINE
Isaiah 28:5–13

'Say, *Please,*' we say to our child. We do not stop if we see no results after twenty-five times. It might be that the twenty-sixth time will bear fruit!

Training should be from birth and must consistently continue throughout life. 'Whom shall he teach knowledge? and whom shall he make to understand doctrine? them that are weaned from the milk, and drawn from the breasts' (28:9). The instruction, correction and admonition required for a frail sinful man to live a productive, consistent and God-honoring life must be taken up by the parent as soon as the infant shows need of learning the lessons of submission and humility! Teachers and church are to follow through. Gradually more and more of the task devolves upon the individual, who must himself bear the responsibility as he matures. It is one continuous process. We call it education in a broad sense. As far as the individual's spiritual growth is involved we call it sanctification.

[148]

'Precept must be upon precept, precept upon precept; line upon line, line upon line; here a little, and there a little' (28:10 and 13). Isaiah repeats his phrases within the verse to demonstrate what he means. Then he even repeats the whole verse, so we can have no excuse for misunderstanding! Repetition is one of the most important keys in the learning process. Never may we be ashamed of it. Patience, tact, understanding and firmness are required on the part of the parent as he trains his child. Similar qualities are required on the part of the maturing adult as he continues his self-discipline. But it is God's way, the way God has used with His frail children all through the years, the method He patiently uses with His frail children today.

This is not a gloomy and monotonous syndrome. This is, really, one of the exciting things about the Christian life! New doors of learning and living are continually opening. They will continue to open until we walk through the gates of heaven itself. Even then we shall surely grow in our knowledge and appreciation of God and His glory through eternity.

RENEWING YOUTH
Isaiah 40:21–31

Some of us are at the point in life when 'the renewal of youth' expresses our precise need. How do we go about meeting this need?

Isaiah admits that at times even God's people faint and become weary. We are at the point of falling, young and old alike. He assures us, however, that God does not faint or grow weary. Power and strength from His own being are poured out upon His people.

Sometimes we experience a mounting up with wings as eagles! God is so near that we feel we might even touch Him. Then it is easy for us to trust. Sometimes we run along amazingly and seem not to be weary at all. He is faithful and His mercies are renewed every morning. Even in dramatically severe times of testing we often are exhilarated and find strength for what seem to be impossible situations.

But what about walking and *not* growing faint? The day-by-day, week-by-week, month-by-month walking is what pulls us down. It is the commuting to work, the household chores, the sleepless nights when a baby cries, and the daily routine which varies very little, that sap our energy.

Here as always we need to take our eyes from self and from circumstances and lift them 'on high' (40:26). When we look to the Creator who is eternally a source of power we may draw from Him all that we need.

George Herbert has a beautiful way of putting this. We must look through the things that would distress us and see the God beyond, rather than fix our eyes on the things themselves:

A man that looks on glass,
    On it may stay his eye,

Or, if he pleaseth, through it pass,
And then the heaven espy.*

Lord, help us to see beyond the visible that would block You out. Give us the ability to see You. Then will our strength be renewed.

Ms.
Isaiah 43:1–7

God has called His people by His name (43:7). What an honor! Ever since the church was planted in Antioch she has delighted as a bride to take the name of her husband—*Christian* (Acts 11:26).

One of the twisted, sad things that we notice today is the reluctance on the part of some women to give up their own surname at marriage. This could be an outward sign of a woman's unwillingness to be truly united to her husband and to become submissive to him. In that case this would be a denial of the one-flesh genius of Christian marriage.

This same independent spirit is manifested in a reluctance to become a member of the organized church, the visible body of Christ.

As we read this section, let us think about the tenderness, the promise of continual faithfulness and love of the Lord the Husband for His wife. Let us think of Calvary, where He died for His

* (The Temple: The Elixir)

[151]

bride, indeed where He died that she might become His bride! Then we can better appreciate what it means to be called by His name.

The Christian woman must be wary of some of the seemingly innocent contemporary trends. She must keep foremost in her thinking the fact that marriage is a beautiful picture of the covenant! A refusal to bear one's husband's name is symptomatic of a reluctance to submit to God's master plan. Surely to attempt to enjoy the advantages of marriage but to refuse its responsibilities is to behave outrageously towards the plan of God for the creatures He made.

We who want to know our identity should be happy to have others know whether we are single or married. Women should be proud to be a Miss or a Mrs., and not let themselves be labelled Ms.! If we are married we should be most happy to bear the name of our husband!

OUR FATHER
Isaiah 64

Humility before God may be said to be the first step in a right relationship toward Him. As we read this chapter we are awed! In the face of such a God we get a true understanding of our own sin. We get, too, an awareness of the sin that infects the whole of our world.

Is there in our homes an awareness of the Sinless One and an awe before Him? Do we see ourselves as creatures sinful in His sight? How is it that, after we have come to this point in our relationship with God, we *dare* reach up boldly to Him? We dare because of the amazing concept we see in verse 8: 'Thou art our Father.' Can you follow this? A sin-laden creature . . . a holy God . . . 'Our Father!'

According to Scripture the answer lies in the grace of this God. It lies in His sending His Son to bear the sins of His people, and in His devising the loving plan by which those who believe in His Son may stand before Him without their sin.

Can our children, as they recognize their own naughtiness or downright defiance and rebellion *dare* to reach out to us simply because they know what it means that we are their father and mother? Are they learning from us what God wants us to understand when He calls Himself our Father?

FEAR
Jeremiah 1:1–10

Our task is not that of Jeremiah. Yet sometimes, as we look at parenthood, we feel that it is too much for us. 'Ah, Lord God! behold, I cannot speak: for I am a child' (1:6). One day our oldest daughter said in jest, but surely out of a heart of real apprehension, 'When our children get into their teens we are going to ship them down to you.'

The task of parenthood comes upon us sud-

[153]

denly, despite the nine months of warning and anticipation. As we look at that little being, a real person whose responsibility has now become ours, all the courses in family living and child psychology, and all the books on raising children, suddenly become inadequate.

Have you known parents who feared their children? Have you known parents who gave up family prayers because their son objected? Or parents who could not refuse something they could not really afford because of temper tantrums that greeted them? Have you known parents who all unawares were taken in by schools of psychology which denied the basic concepts of God's Word? Have you known parents who read only the parts of God's Word which speak of love, skimming over those which speak of discipline? It takes real courage to be a parent.

What does God say to Jeremiah? 'Whatsoever I command thee thou shalt speak. Be not afraid of their faces . . .' (1:7,8). Parents need courage from God. We are to follow His directions for child-rearing and leave the rest in His hands. His words must be in our mouth. The faces of sulkiness, of pleading, of tears, of rebellion are not to cause us to fear. Our strength is in the Lord!

EXPECTING OBEDIENCE
Jeremiah 35:12–19

Jonadab the son of Rechab has a unique place in Scripture. He is used as an example to teach obedience to God. Jonadab told his sons not to drink wine. No details are given. God wants us to concentrate on the father's command and the children's obedience. The sons obey their father. That is the significant thing.

When we issue a command, do we realize that we are ruling for God? Do we consider ourselves channels through which His authority is directed? Parents have no right to arrogate to themselves an authority in the home. They are to recognize that any authority they have rests solely in the plan of God for the government of the home.

This is an awesome thing! It means we need to be sure of our commands and requirements. We need to take care that we do not command out of adherence to the traditions of men, or out of habit, or because of the way we ourselves were reared, or because of what the world thinks. Our requirements for the home must be squarely based upon the Word of God.

When we command with a sense of these facts we are to expect to be obeyed. We are to insist upon being obeyed. There may not be a timidity, an apology for the command. The concept of the law of God and the obedience man owes Him is at stake here. From the way we govern our own children, they and the world will learn what a Sovereign God is and what it is to be His people.

CRYING IN THE NIGHT
Lamentations 2:17–22

Israel had sinned. God in His just anger had punished His people. What a terrifying scene Jeremiah paints here!

There was heartache and distress all about the city. There was physical pain and anguish and hunger of which we in our favored country cannot conceive. Above all there was the anguish of soul that is even more unbearable.

No wonder the parents were to 'arise and cry out in the night' before the Lord for their young children (2:19). One version reads this way:

> Arise, cry aloud in the night
> At the beginning of the night watches;
> Pour out your heart like water
> Before the presence of the Lord;
> Lift up your hands to Him
> For the life of your little ones
> Who are faint because of hunger
> At the head of every street. (NASV)

Today our children hunger for truth. There is anguish and pain of spirit. There is estrangement and defeat. On every side they are being fed husks which will not nourish their souls. To the sensitive Christian, today is as terrifying as was the day of Jeremiah! When did we last cry aloud in the beginning of the watches and pour out our hearts like water before the face of the Lord for the life of our young children that faint in hunger in the top of every street?

Lord, teach us as a Christian community to pray like that for our children, our grandchildren, children all over the world! Help us to give them the food they need for their souls!

YOKES FOR YOUTH
Lamentations 3:22–41

'It is good for a man that he bear the yoke in his youth' says Jeremiah in verse 27. This yoke, as we may judge from the context, probably referred directly to subjection to a foreign power. What a statement! Captivity good? That is what God says. As we study this portion we see that the yoke, the reproach, the grief, the suffering that we are caused to bear are means of driving us to our God who all along has been faithful and is not allowing us to endure this without purpose. His compassions do not fail. They are new every morning. Great is His faithfulness (3:22,23)!

What does this verse say to parents today? We need to recognize that our children do have yokes to bear in their youth. So far we have not had to endure subjection to foreign powers, but children do have physical problems, social stigma, homework, rules and regulations imposed upon them, and disappointments. These can be heavy burdens. They are limitations of freedom that parallel in the experience of the child the captivity of Israel!

Are these good for the child? How? They teach him the pattern of life with its vicissitudes. They teach him that the world does not revolve around *him* and that there will not always be smiles of approval to greet his cute speeches or pillows spread out to cushion his falls. They give the child a realistic view of himself and the sinful world about him.

Sometimes we as parents attempt to remove completely normal types of hardship from our children's ways. We are loath to see them have to wait or have to do without things they want. We feel sorry when things do not always go their way. We should capitalize on these experiences! We should say, 'Thank You, Lord, for enabling this child to grow. Thank You for providing him with this beautiful evidence of your faithfulness in adversity!'

It is difficult to see our children bear yokes, but let us not always be trying to protect them! Let us use the opportunity to point them to Jesus whose yoke is easy!

THUS SAITH THE LORD
Ezekiel 2:1–8

As Christians we glory in the truth that each believer is a prophet, a priest and a king. Yet often we do not act like prophets and priests and kings in our own homes where these offices have a special significance.

As a prophet, the parent proclaims God's truth to his children. As a priest, he brings his children before God in prayer. As a king, he rules them wisely in God's ways.

Or does he? What happens when he faces the rebellion of his children? Doesn't he all too often throw up his hands and say, 'What's the use?' or 'I can't do anything with him!'

What does Ezekiel have to say to this situation? His remarks are very appropriate and forceful. We are to say, 'Thus says the Lord God. And they, whether they will hear, or whether they will forbear (for they are a rebellious house,) yet shall know that there hath been a prophet among them' (2:4,5).

Parents, if we fail to obey God in this important matter, we need ourselves to be pointed to God's Word! God instructs us in Chapter 2, verses 7 and 8 and Chapter 3, verse 4: 'Be not *thou* rebellious like that rebellious house.' Failure to be a prophet in our home is itself rebellion against God!

The father needs to proclaim God's truth to his children fearlessly. And as he does this he needs to pray for them and to lead them by his life and direction into the way of the Lord.

NOAH, DANIEL AND JOB
Ezekiel 14:12–23

This is a strangely potent passage of Scripture. God tells us of desolation that He will send because of the sins of the people. He says He will send famine and animal hordes and the sword and pestilence. As these words are being written our news media is warning us of food and energy shortages ahead. The thought of polluted air and water frightens us. We are alarmed at the percentage of unemployed. Other problems loom large on our horizon. Have we considered the possibility that these might be punishments from God for the sins of the people?

God implies that in such a time some men might be delivered from this destruction—men who are faithful to Him such as Noah and Daniel and Job. But they could only deliver themselves!

God's Word warns very boldly that no one will be spared because of his father's righteousness! There is no treasury of merit. Each man will stand or fall because of his own righteousness or his own sin in the sight of God. 'Though . . . Noah, Daniel, and Job, were in it (the land) they should deliver but their own souls . . . they shall deliver neither sons nor daughters' (14:14,16).

One day one of our daughters was heard comforting her sister thus, 'Don't worry. You won't go to hell, because our father is a minister.' We had better be careful that our children realize that God deals with each of us individually!

But again God shows Himself gracious! In verse 22 He promises that yet there will be a remnant, both sons and daughters. They will serve Jehovah and they will be a comfort to the older people of God.

What a beautiful conclusion: 'Ye shall know that I have not done without cause all that I have done in it, saith the Lord God' (14:23). Everything our God does is intentional, purposeful. It all hangs together. We shall see the whole pattern some day and rejoice!

A BABY AND A BRIDE
Ezekiel 16:1–14

Again God speaks to His people through His prophet concerning their sin. Here He expresses Himself through images drawn from family life. Through them He reminds His people of His love for them down through the years.

In verses 3–6 He speaks of His people as a newborn baby, navel uncut, unwashed, not cleaned with salt, not carefully wrapped, but rather cast out in an open field to perish with no one to pity! God reminds them that He took compassion upon the baby and cared for her, nurturing her until she was grown up and mature.

Then in verses 7–14 God speaks of His people as a mature young woman whom He has washed and arrayed in fine clothing and jewels. In verse 8 He speaks of actually making her His bride. How could God explain to us more clearly

His love for us, and our dependence upon His grace for all that we are? In this remarkable passage we see in small compass the rich imagery of the father's love and care for his child (even an adopted child) and of the husband's love and care for his wife! We see, too, a powerful demonstration of the truth found later in the New Testament: 'Marriage is honorable in all, and the bed undefiled' (Hebrews 13:4). O God, thank You for Your love!

LIKE MOTHER, LIKE DAUGHTER
Ezekiel 16:44–63

Some of us are shocked on occasion to look into the mirror and be greeted by a remarkable resemblance to our father or mother! What an amazing phenomenon—a cast of the eye, a tilt of the head, a curl of the lip! 'As is the mother, so is her daughter' (16:44).

More awesome it is to see traits of character, and sins, in ourselves that we have seen, perhaps with some disgust, in our parents. The same things about which we used to be critical persist in cropping up in ourselves.

Sometimes God's people see the sins of their *unbelieving* parents getting a hold in their own lives. 'Yet hast thou not walked after their ways, nor done after their abominations: but, as if that were a very little thing, thou wast corrupted more than they in all thy ways' (16:47). As Christians so much more is expected of us! Yet here we are falling into sins that our parents were subject to, sometimes even sinking lower than they did, at least from the point of view of privilege.

We should be bowing our heads in shame and pleading for God's forgiveness. 'Like mother, like daughter' is all very well when it comes to physical appearances, abilities or good qualities. When we are God's children, however, we may not repeat the sins of our parents in our own lives. If our parents are unbelievers this is even more shameful.

How thankful, Lord, we are for the latter verses in this chapter. You will remember Your covenant, despite our unfaithfulness (16:60).

BALANCE
Ezekiel 18:19–32

Is it not very exhilarating to read this chapter?

In the Decalogue we see how the sins of the fathers are felt down through the years by generations that follow. It is easy to point out from our own experience illustrations of this fact. Likewise we read of the blessings that accrue to the children and grandchildren of godly persons. We praise God today, too, for His faithfulness to the children of the covenant.

But balanced over against this teaching is the truth that men are responsible persons whose dignity is to be respected. As we saw in Ezekiel 14, so we see here: each one must account for his own life. Being born in a Christian home is not a guarantee of personal salvation. There is nothing automatic about the covenant. Parents might wish sometimes that this were the case, but that would be to cheapen God's plan and to dwarf mankind.

Conversely, though, being born into an ungodly home will not automatically result in a man's damnation, nor is it an excuse for his unbelief. God rejoices when the wicked turn from their ways and live! He has no pleasure in their death, but He does require personal commitment to Himself that they might live.

We need to maintain the balance of Scripture between God's electing grace and man's responsibility, between covenant promises and the individual's obligation for personal commitment. A failure to maintain this balance is a misrepresentation of God's truth as He has clearly revealed it. Such failure can cause a person to plunge into unwholesome extremes and distort the perspective of Scripture.

SELF-DISCIPLINE
Daniel 1:1–16

The Hebrew youths who took such a strong stand in the court of the king of Babylon are a tribute to fathers and mothers who faithfully trained them in the home. They are a testimony to the keeping power of their God. Chosen to be educated in the court of the conqueror along with the children of the king himself and the children of princes! Given to eat of the delicacies of the king's table! Children outstanding in appearance, intelligent, well-educated, full of promise! They were to be taught 'the learning and the tongue of the Chaldeans' (1:4).

This was a difficult spot in which to be. Not only did they experience social pressures such as our children experience in kindergarten or in college or in military service; there were, too, the powers of an unsympathetic 'administration.' This is a story to which our youth should be able to relate!

It would have been very easy to capitulate to the life style of the Babylonians. It would have been a temptation to compete for first place among the youth at the court. It would have been the easiest course to adapt to the Chaldean style of life. But God was with them. He enabled them to hold out against the ways that would have compromised their faith. Then He went a step further and enabled them to surpass all the others!

We may assume that, back home, parents were praying for God's care over these boys. They had done what they could in training them. Now the discipline had to be in the hands of the youths themselves. Away from the parental apron-strings they would have to maintain their own faith and relationship to the God of their fathers. We believe the parents prayed to this end.

So, too, must we.

THEY FOUND DANIEL PRAYING
Daniel 6

Daniel could be counted on. The king's men knew that he would be praying three times a day to his God. Often they had walked by his house and seen through the window this man on his knees giving thanks to his God. They wanted to catch him in something that would discredit him before the king. An attack on his prayer life was a strategy they knew would be sure to succeed.

What if it were actually decreed that no one must pray to any but the king? What would Daniel do? They were confident that Daniel would continue faithfully to pray to the King of heaven and earth.

As people of God we pray daily and give thanks to our Saviour. What if Congress should decree that such behaviour was anti-American, and that we must now direct any requests to our local governmental agencies? What if we were subject to fine or imprisonment for praying to God? What would we do then?

The church has such an easy time in America today! Do we give thanks for this? Do we pour out our gratitude to the King of kings daily for His grace in granting us such liberty of worship? Do we thank Him for delivering us from the bondage of sin?

Do we gather with His people to pray, regularly, so that if the local police wanted us they would know where to find us on Sunday morning and at other times when the church assembles for worship?

GOD'S PROPHET MARRIES A HARLOT
Hosea 1

The book of Hosea, like the Song of Solomon, is a source of embarrassment to some of God's people. Elsewhere in Scripture we read, 'Thou shalt not commit adultery . . . Whosoever shall marry her that is divorced committeth adultery' (Matthew 5:27,32). But in this book God actually commands His prophet Hosea to take for his wife a harlot! What are we to think about that?

Some would solve the problem by claiming that this was a dream or vision that Hosea had. They cannot accept it as a completely factual or historical account. But the straightforward way in which it is written makes that position untenable. It is very difficult to avoid the force of the facts as they come to us here.

Does this book not demonstrate again in a most effective manner God's use of *imagery* to teach sinful, ignorant human beings His truth? Here in the life story of one of His own prophets He demonstrates the high regard He has for marriage and His abhorrence of adultery. He is pre-eminently revealing to men then and now the Eternal Bridegroom who is so patient with His bride, even when she has played the harlot and departed from Him in unbelief.

'And I will betroth you to me for ever; Yea, I will betroth you to me in righteousness and in justice, in lovingkindness and in compassion, and I will betroth you to me in faithfulness. Then you will know the Lord' (Hosea 2:19,20 NASB).

TELL YOUR SONS
Joel 1:1–10

The locusts swarmed down upon the land and devastated it. Our encounters with the seventeen-year locust give us a little inkling of this destruction. The description in Joel of the land's encounter with this pestilence is vivid indeed.

God speaks to His people at this time through Joel. He wants them to take notice and learn from experience. He says, 'Tell ye your children of it, and let your children tell their children, and their children another generation' (1:3).

What has God taught us in the hard places of life? Has He caused us to go through deep waters in order to cast us upon Himself for mercy and comfort? Has He brought afflictions upon us to humble us or to teach us what it is to be completely driven into His arms, having nothing else upon which we might rest?

Then we must be humble and open enough with our children to tell them these experiences of the might, the power, the judgment and the loving forgiveness of our heavenly Father. God wants us to enable them to participate in our experience. He does not want His lessons forgotten. He does not want to have to repeat them every generation. Nor do we want Him to, do we?

PUNISHMENT INDICATES LOVE!
Amos 3:1–11

Punishment must be regarded by God's people as a sign that we stand in a special relationship to Him: 'You only have I known of all the families of the earth; therefore I will punish you for all your iniquities' (3:2).

We have previously pointed out that the word *to know* in the languages of Scripture does not mean simply *to recognize* or have *cognizance of.* It means *to love.* Because God loved Israel He punished her! Punishment in this context is an evidence of caring. If parents do not care what trouble their children get into or how badly they mess up their lives and the lives of others, if they do not care to what extent their children will incur the wrath of God, then they need not go through all the emotional anguish of punishing and training and disciplining. Parents who love their children *must* punish them and point them to God.

Can two walk together except they be agreed? (3:3). God wants us to be able to walk with Him, to have day-by-day fellowship with Him. This we cannot do if we are estranged. Because He

[169]

loves us and wants us to be able to walk with Him, He punishes our sin. This punishment is designed to alert us to our sin and its seriousness and to bring us back to the path of obedience. This punishment is for our sanctification.

God does not punish us so that we may thereby pay for the wrong we have done or atone for our sins! This we can never do. This we need never do, either. God sent His Son to do this for us. And His Son willingly came and obtained our redemption.

Thank You, God, for Your great plan! Thank You for loving us enough to save us. Thank You for loving us enough to punish us and to sanctify us so that we may walk with You!

THE WIFE OF YOUR YOUTH
Malachi 2:1–17

The leaving of God for false gods was the sin of the Israelites generation after generation. Malachi addresses himself to this in a general way. Here at the beginning of this chapter he warns the priests against causing men to stumble at the law.

Then the prophet takes up God's favorite imagery and says that Judah has married the daughter of a strange god (2:11). In the fashion we have grown used to, he interweaves closely the heavenly and the earthly, swinging over from a statement of the sin of the people of Judah as a whole to sin in specific personal relationships. He condemns roundly the man who leaves the godly wife of his youth and marries another, an unbeliever, as He condemns the nation for forsaking its God.

Commentators vary in their handling of verse 15, but obviously it is underlining the divine requirement for God's people: one man and one woman who serve Him and who in their marriage provide the context for a godly seed.

In verses 15 and 16 notice the repetition of the word *spirit*. Not only is the outward deed of forsaking the wife of your youth (or the God of your youth) sinful; the very attitude of mind must be that of fidelity. The lustful look condemned by Jesus in the Sermon on the Mount is sin. God is concerned with the life of the spirit.

One God, one people. One husband, one wife. The same theme from Genesis to Malachi and on to Revelation! Any variations are an affront to the Creator and spell havoc in the lives of the offenders as well as in the generations that follow. Infractions of God's perfect law have repercussions which are felt throughout society.

ROBBING GOD
Malachi 3:6–12

A mother in the Dutch tradition used to say to her family, 'A tenth for the church, a tenth for the Christian school and we'll live on the rest.' We do not need in our day to belabor the fact that in setting up a home a couple needs to make plans for financial security. What we do need to stress is that a couple need also from the beginning of marriage to take God into their financial plans and honour Him with the firstfruits of their income (Proverbs 3:9).

In the Old Testament economy it is abundantly plain that God required a tithe of one's income. Jesus affirmed this. Although in the New Testament the expression is rarely used, the principle is never abrogated. God does not wish us to be legalistic in our giving. He wants us, using the Old Testament tithe as a base, to offer up even more, in accordance with our ability, out of love and gratitude for the gift of His greatest treasure, His own Son.

Do we take Him at His word when He says that He will open the windows of heaven and pour out upon us a blessing we shall not have room to receive (3:10)? We realize, don't we, that this blessing from heaven may be material riches, but, more precious still, it may be spiritual riches. We love this verse and its promise!

But what about verse 9: 'Ye are cursed with a curse: for ye have robbed me, even this whole nation'?

THE BOOK OF REMEMBRANCE
Malachi 3:13–18

Some young Christians in this generation have a freedom in speaking often to one another about the Lord which some of their parents from a more reserved day have to achieve with some effort. God is pleased if we speak often 'one to another' about Him (3:16). That is part of what Deuteronomy 6 is all about. Especially in the home should we manifest God's reality and presence by speaking freely about Him.

Verses 14 and 15 point to the person who thinks the long-faced Christian has done his duty. In verse 16 it is made clear that those in whom the fear of the Lord really flourishes will bubble over in their love and praise and very naturally share together their faith and testimony to His grace. He will hear them and engrave their names in His Book of Remembrance!

Those people He will spare as a man spares his faithful son. They will be gathered up into His safe treasury in the day when He will come to make up His jewels. Others may perish but these will be safe.

O God, unloosen our tongues! We think about You so often, but our conversation does not reflect our thoughts. We are like Gamaliel Bradford:

> I think about God,
>   Yet I talk of small matters.
> Now isn't it odd
>   How my idle tongue chatters!
> Of quarrelsome neighbors,
>   Fine weather and rain,
> Indifferent labors,
>   Indifferent pain,

Some trivial style
    Fashion shifts with a nod.
And yet all the while
    I am thinking of God.*

Help us together to seek to give You Your place in our daily conversation.

REMEMBER GOD'S LAW
Malachi 4:1–6

What is John the Baptist (coming in the spirit of Elijah) going to do? What does Malachi mean when he says that John is going to turn the hearts of the parents and children to each other? Is he going to destroy the generation gap?

When the gospel of repentance and faith in the Saviour which John began to proclaim takes hold in a home it does indeed do away with the generation gap! In the home committed to Christ there is peace. There are no struggles for supremacy. The humble parent seeks to lead the child in God's way. The obedient child delights to be led. There is openness and communication. All speak the truth in love. This is embraced in the prophecy of Malachi.

In a special sense, too, the fathers of the faith, the Old Testament stalwarts, are to be thought of as being turned to the children who will be

* *Shadow Verses.* Yale University Press, 1920.

[174]

coming to God from the other side of Calvary. Together, we all by God's Spirit are facing our Father in heaven as a unified family.

As we are about to enter the New Testament era Malachi gives us the formula for holy living as the family of God: Remember God's law. Grace will be poured out in a new way at the cross and at Pentecost but the law will not be abandoned. It has permanent use as a revelation of God's nature. It shows us our sins and acts as a schoolmaster to drive us to Christ. And it is His appointed guide for holy living appropriate in His family.

Remember God's law!

THE FAMILY OF JESUS
Matthew 1:1–17

The Old Testament opens with the creation of the first man, Adam. The New Testament opens with the incarnation of the second Adam, God's Son, our Lord Jesus Christ. In Adam all died. All those in Christ are made alive.

Why this genealogy? What is God teaching us by beginning the New Testament with a family tree which we have difficulty in reading, and especially aloud? God is teaching us at least three things in this chapter. It is very important for us to understand what they are.

First, He is teaching us that Jesus is a real human being. God is rooting Jesus firmly in space-time. He is completely eliminating the possibility of our being swept away into some extra-historical view of our Saviour. Jesus is truly man just as certainly as He is truly God.

Second, God is pointing out in a striking fashion that His normal way of working is within the framework of the family. The family is His point of reference. The family is the backbone of society. As we review the lives of some of the persons in this family tree we are aghast at God's grace in including them in the genealogy of His Son! But there they are! The family is the normal channel through which God works.

And third, God is showing us how He miraculously preserved the line of promise all the way from creation. The barrenness of Sarah, the captivity of the Jews, the machinations of Haman—nothing hindered His purpose to send His Son. Christ's genealogy is a reminder of this!

We thank You, God, for all Your Word, even for the 'begats.'

THE SUPERNATURAL
Matthew 1:18–25

In recent years we have gained more respect for the supernatural. With a resurgence of the evidence of the reality of demonic powers, Christians are becoming less apologetic for their belief in the powers of God that transcend the natural. This is a shameful admission to have to make but there appears to be a good deal of truth to it.

The events of the birth of Christ are steeped in the supernatural. God preserved the line of promise supernaturally. When the time came for the Messiah to appear He was miraculously conceived in the womb of the virgin. Then, as we read here, God in His tenderness ministered to the needs of the just man, Joseph, who was much distressed to find his betrothed with child, by supernaturally revealing to him an explanation of the cause of her pregnancy.

All these happenings, the timing, the circumstances, occurred as a part of the symphony God had been composing all through the years, the design He had been sketching in the Old Testament prophecies. The prophecy fulfilled in verse 23 was uttered some 750 years previously. Surely this transcends the natural!

The God we worship governs all things. He is over and above the natural, not bound by the laws He made to govern the natural world. Nothing is too hard for Him.

This is the God with whom we have to do. Let us take courage.

A BABY IS BORN
Matthew 2:1–12

A baby is born. Gifts are brought. There is great joy. This is so completely within our experience that we respond to it readily.

And this is Christmas! Christmas, celebrated with love and reverence and thanksgiving to God for His gift, is a beautiful time in the Christian family.

Let us keep our Christmas. Let us not relinquish it to the world. God's love in giving us His Son makes our heart sing. We want to say 'Thank You' in a special way. We want to sing the carols which celebrate His love.

We, in turn, want to give. Out of hearts overflowing with gratitude we want to give something special to God. We want to share what we have with others, those in need, those dear to us.

True, Christmas has been prostituted by the world. Ours is the challenge to keep it simple and beautiful in our own lives and homes. Because sex has been poisoned by the world, do we throw out sex? Because God's Day has been largely taken over for business and pleasure, do we fail to keep it, too?

It is a challenge to have a truly Christian Christmas, stripped of pagan tradition and ungodly celebration. As we who are Christians strive to keep our Christmas Christian, this could be in the years ahead a striking testimony to others of our faith in the God who sent His Son to die that His people might live.

'They worshipped him,' says verse 11 concerning the wise men. And they brought Him gifts. Have you seen the car bumper sticker: 'Wise men still worship Him'? It is a sign of wisdom to worship the Saviour, wisdom which is a gift of God.

FIDELITY
Matthew 5:27-32

The baby has grown up to be a man, the God-man. In this chapter He is preaching His best-known sermon, The Sermon on the Mount. It is of much profit to see how the teachings here harmonize with and complement the teachings we read from the Old Testament.

The Lord Jesus speaks out severely against adultery. The simple words of the Eighth Commandment, 'Thou shalt not commit adultery' were amplified in the Tenth Commandment to include even the coveting of our neighbor's wife, so this strong denunciation of both the adulterous deed and desire should not surprise us. The Saviour saw the need of emphasizing the inward aspects of the command, which had been neglected during the previous centuries. Attitudes are the basic subject of this part of his discourse. It is from these that actions spring.

This section underlines, too, the exclusiveness of marriage: one man and one woman until death! This allows for no temporary arrangements, no trial marriages, no triangles of any kind. The truly Christian marriage calls for complete fidelity, even of the inner man. The relationship in such a marriage is one of voluntary faithfulness and complete freedom from concern over the faithfulness of the partner.

Are we as the Bride of Christ as true to Him

as our relationship requires? Great is *His* faithfulness. What about *ours?*

PATER NOSTER
Matthew 6:1–15

Through the years probably the most repeated prayer in the Christian Church has been the one the Saviour taught His disciples to pray, the *Pater Noster,* the 'Our Father.'

How many who glibly repeat this prayer have taken note of the way in which Jesus uses the possessive adjective *our?* Look back to verse 6 and see where He tells the believer to pray to 'thy Father.' Then in verse 8 He speaks to them concerning 'your Father.' As He presents the sample or model prayer in verse 9 he bids them pray, 'Our Father.' Do you see that He is nowhere classifying Himself with them as being children of God together in the same sense. He is being scrupulous about this!

More striking still is the scene in the garden outside the empty tomb. He tells Mary not to touch Him. He says, 'I ascend unto my Father and your Father; and to my God, and your God' (John 20:17). Within the Trinity there is God the Father and there is Jesus Christ, the Son. Scripture tells us that Jesus is the only-begotten Son of the Father. At the same time, as one of the persons of the Trinity, Jesus is Himself God! In that mysterious unity and diversity Christ assures us of His eternal Sonship and at the same time of His voluntary submission to the eternal Father.

We cannot be allowed to regard our Father and our God in the same way that Jesus does! We who are sinful creatures can call God 'our Father' only by His grace. We have become His children by adoption, through His act of love in giving His only-begotten Son to die on our behalf.

When the world would vainly attempt to humanize God the Son, Christians must be very careful to maintain the distinction He has drawn. Jesus did not pray the Lord's prayer, but by His life and death He made it possible for us to pray it! Our Father! Pater Noster!

A FATHER'S GIFTS
Matthew 7:7–12

It is not normal for love to remain penned up within us, unexpressed. It needs to express itself in some way. In Scripture one of the ways in which we frequently see fathers expressing love for their children is by giving. In this they are but following the example set by God the Father.

This section speaks of the good gifts fathers give to their children. To know how our heavenly Father gives to His children who ask is an encouragement to pray. Elsewhere we see specifically that He will give the Holy Spirit to those who ask. The Holy Spirit is God Himself! God will give Himself to His children who ask.

Do we really give our children what they ask

for? When possible we do. Do we give them the attention they are asking for when they quietly slip into the room while we are reading? Do we give them time they tacitly ask for from our busy schedule? Do we give them teaching they ask for when they express doubts and uncertainty? Do we give them the correction and punishment they 'ask for' when they are disobedient? Are we really expressing our love for our children by our gifts?

What about ourselves as children of God? How much do we ask of our Father? Our children should be learning by our example to ask God for the good gifts He has promised to give. How vital is prayer in our home? We should give evidence that we really expect our heavenly Father to hear and answer our prayers according to His power and good pleasure.

What are we waiting for?

WHO IS MY MOTHER?
Matthew 12:46–50

Mary has been called by some 'the mother of God' but Protestants would rather refer to her as the 'mother of Jesus,' since this term is specific concerning the God-given position she occupied. By grace she was granted to participate in the incarnation of the second person of the Trinity.

In Matthew 12 we read an interesting sentiment from the lips of Jesus. He appears to be shedding any claims His mother might have upon Him! He had been subject to her and to Joseph as He was growing up. Now that He has embarked upon His public ministry He wants it known that His relationship to Mary is no different from His relationship to you and to me!

We can suppose that, since Mary was truly a human mother, this pierced her heart as a sword. Mothers often have a real struggle relinquishing their hold upon their maturing sons and daughters. Many times they deeply resent that other woman who has come into the life of their son or that man who has robbed them of the close mother-daughter relationship they used to enjoy.

Jesus was not being cruel. In a very striking way He was teaching the great truth that all believers are precious to Him! Each one is a sister or mother or brother for whom He died! He is not relegating Mary to a low place. He is raising us to a high one with her. We can believe that He honored her all his life, even on the cross when He lovingly entrusted her to the care of John.

A word to the husband of a woman who is finding it difficult to see her son go! This is a time when you should lovingly insist that she untie those apron strings. Your wife, in whom emotion is such a driving force, may be blinded to what she is doing to this son, to herself and to you. Your strength is needed here. If you fail to step in, the son himself may some day have to break this tie. That would be much more difficult and not nearly so appropriate.

[183]

A man is to leave his mother as he assumes responsibility for a new family unit. Yes, mother, his leaving may hurt, but as you face it with Christ you can grow!

WHO IS THE GREATEST?
Matthew 18:1–14

In vaulting ambition the disciples inquired of Jesus, 'Who is greatest in the kingdom of heaven?' Jesus called a child and set him in their midst. Then He preached a sermon on humility, emphasizing the need of turning from sin and demonstrating a child-like faith. Such an attitude of heart, He told them, is one of the evidences of being born again.

'Whoever therefore shall humble himself as this little child, the same is greatest in the kingdom of heaven.' The humility which Jesus Himself showed in being born as a man and in enduring the cross, He asks us to display. This humility which is characteristic of a child will yield honor in heaven. The man who is humble before God will be called great in heaven.

Even now, Jesus tells us, the angels which God has assigned to the special guardianship of the children of His love are looking upon the face of the heavenly Father. One eye, we might say, is on the child to protect him from harm and one eye is upon the Father to beseech His aid. God in His grace has made special provision for the children of His love.

[184]

It is not the will or pleasure of God 'that one of these little ones should perish.' How precious is this to the parent! And how illuminating it is to glimpse this aspect of God who delights in humility and who honors the humble!

GIVEN TO GOD
Mark 7:1–13

The Scribes and Pharisees were zealous to keep the laws of the Old Testament, but their zeal extended also to the manufacture of other laws, 'the traditions of the elders,' which had been heaped up in addition and which they were most scrupulous in obeying. Jesus had to admonish them for this sin of heaping up laws and placing them as a burden on the people. Our reading illustrates this. Specifically here He warns them against the gift that was *corban*. Just what did that mean?

In the Ten Commandments God had said that men should 'honor their father and mother' (Exodus 20:12). He who did not, but rather cursed his parents, would be guilty and deserving of death. When this responsibility to honor and care for needy and elderly parents became irksome, men devised ways (quite pious ways!) of circumventing God's command. They gave, or probably sometimes only pretended that they gave, a gift to God and said, 'This is corban' ('brought near,' that is to say, given to God). The gift would pass into the hands of the scribes and Pharisees for their use, and the needy parents would gain nothing by it. Thus was God's law set aside and God's name dishonored.

God did not want such a gift. Rather, He would have the son honor his parents, as the law required. Jesus found it necessary to condemn *corban* as a pure circumvention of the divine will.

We are told elsewhere that normally it is the parent who should lay up for the child, but we are also told to take care of our own. Special instructions are given for the care of widows in our families. When aged parents are in need, God surely requires us to care for them as best we can.

This is not to be construed simply in monetary ways. The aged parent is cheered not only by gifts but by the knowledge that someone cares. We should seek grace from the Lord to recognize the needs of older people and to respond to them. In our day the Social Security program has come to be depended upon as a mainstay for aging people. God has his own program for social security built into His kingdom. Are we concerned to see that it functions to His glory?

LET THE CHILDREN COME*
Mark 10:13–16

Children are important to Jesus. He had time specially for them. He even rebuked those who

* RSV.

would keep the children from Him. Jesus, the Creator, was aware that children are tomorrow's men and women. They are each important to their Creator.

Here again we read a tender incident in the life of Jesus which gives evidence of how important little children are to Him. The mothers wanted Him to 'touch' them. And He did! 'He took them up in his arms, put his hands upon them, and blessed them.' The touch of Jesus expressed closeness, love and unity.

So often we fail to recognize the capacity of children for real saving faith, despite the words of Jesus in Matthew 18:6 where He speaks of 'these little ones which believe in me.' We are reluctant to receive children as professing members of the church at an early age. This has proven a wise procedure in that it may forestall premature professions on the part of those who have not had their faith tested by even a slight brush with unbelief. But we must be cautious. Children at an early age *can* exercise a saving faith. In the home and church we should honor and nourish that faith and not be guilty of keeping children away from Jesus. Their qualities which Jesus held forth do equip them for acceptance of the Saviour and growth in Him. And Jesus has in His grace declared, 'Of such is the kingdom of heaven.'

As a church are we concerned to provide for the needs of the covenant children? Are we concerned to reach the children of our neighborhood for the Saviour? Our poor example or our indifference may be as effective as the rebukes of the disciples in keeping the young away from the house of God. And, as Jesus said, it would be better to have a millstone around one's neck than to offend 'one of these little ones which believe in me.'

A GODLY COUPLE
Luke 1:1–6

After God spoke through Malachi there were some four hundred years when there was no revelation to men from their Creator. What was happening through these years?

There was much apostasy. Many turned from the precepts of God. Many failed to obey God's command to remember His law, as we find it written in Malachi's closing chapter (4:4).

There were some, however, who through the generations were still faithful to God. They had taught their children as God had required. They had prayed. They were waiting in faith for the Messiah to come. In the midst of those who were asking scornfully 'Where is the promise of his coming?', there were some whose eyes were turned toward the future and whose ears were awaiting the angelic announcement.

Zacharias was one of the latter. He was a faithful priest in the temple in Jerusalem. His wife, Elizabeth, also of priestly descent, shared his hope. 'They were both righteous before God, walking in all the commandments and ordinances of the Lord blameless' (Luke 1:6). They were

[188]

not perfect, but their lives were marked by godliness.

The beautiful picture of marriage we have here in Zacharias and Elizabeth reminds us that there is a unity of spirit that can exist only with two believing persons. Two unbelievers joined in marriage worship gods of their own making. In a mixed marriage obviously each is worshipping a different god. In Christian marriage a man and a woman are walking hand in hand in the same direction, both of them fully resolved to obey the God of their salvation according to His Word. There is possible for the Christian couple a relationship which none else can have.

Are we both Christians? Are we experiencing what would be possible for us if each were living in close fellowship with God? Do our own children or grandchildren, or the children of others, see in us what God can make of a marriage like that of Zacharias and Elizabeth? As in their day, men now ask in scorn, 'where is the promise of his coming?' (2 Peter 3:4). Do we live holy lives that anticipate the return of our Saviour?

DISGRACE!
Luke 1:7–25

'To take away my disgrace among men!' How amazing this statement sounds to today's ears! This is completely out of harmony with current thought-patterns. Today many women consider it quite within their right and prerogative to choose to be childless. This choice is now within a woman's power and she can use one of various means to prevent herself from becoming a mother. If her precautions fail she can abort the child who has begun to grow in her womb.

So it is indeed strange to think of childlessness as being a disgrace among men! But that is the way it was in Bible days. Children were considered an heritage of the Lord. The fruit of the womb was His reward. Children were called 'arrows' in the 'quiver' of a man and he was happy when his 'quiver' was full (Psalm 127:3–5).

Of course there was no population explosion at that time. Children were needed to help with the chores. Besides, it was not so easy to prevent having them. Today children may be a real burden financially. It isn't even considered moral or patriotic to have a large family! One could really become alarmed by listening to prognostications concerning food shortages, pollution, and inflation in the future. Parents might well be apprehensive concerning the hardships today's babies will probably experience during their life-span.

'But God . . . ,' as Martyn Lloyd-Jones reminds us. He comments that many of the things that the world says, are true; our situation is frightening; yes, we must agree. 'But God . . .' Here is the difference. God wants to bless us with children. His estimate of their value is the accurate one. Surely the world needs as much of the salt of Christian faith as we can supply. There may be overpopulation, but there will never be overpopulation of Christians. There may be increasing pollution of the material world, but the influence of Christians is needed to counteract the more serious pollution of morals. Furthermore, the projected woes of the future will never be too severe for the one whose God is the Lord!

THE VIRGIN BIRTH
Luke 1:26–38

There was a time when you could use the doctrine of the virgin birth of Christ as a gauge of faithfulness to the teachings of the Scriptures. A man might hedge on or spiritualize many of the teachings of Scripture in order to be able to assent to them and yet at the same time entertain mental reservations about their authenticity. But the virgin birth? There was only one thing you could say about that: a woman gave birth to a child without having had intercourse.

The day we have described has passed. Now the Christian has to be more wary in accepting the word of theologians at large. The virgin birth itself can be assented to without being regarded as we have described it. There is a whole widening school of thought which would claim that this event, along with many of the other events of Scripture which we hold dear, occurred in a different plane. Their truth is not denied. It is just said that they happened on a different historical plane.

'I cannot understand that,' you say. Neither can we. But many claim that they can, simply because they refuse to believe that God's Word is everywhere true.

To the Christian, however, the virgin birth is the perfect answer to God's dilemma! He wanted to send into the world One who was fully God, in order that His perfect life and substitutionary death might be of infinite value and become the groundwork of salvation. And He Himself was the eternal Father of the eternal Son. He wanted to send forth One who was fully man, so that He could really represent us. He chose a human being to give birth to the Son whom He sent from heaven. It is beautiful! It is so integral to the Christian faith that to remove it from the Bible is to do violence to the perfect scheme of God.

We cannot accept the Barthian view expressed in paragraph two. Nor can we understand how such a conception as Isaiah prophesied (7:14) and Matthew and Luke define, could take place. Mary could not understand either, but she sang in verse 37, '. . . with God nothing shall be impossible!'

WOMAN-TALK
Luke 1:39–56

What an amazing conversation these two women had together! They had bonds between them that gave them a freedom to speak of what was on their hearts. They were cousins and both pregnant for the first time. They were pregnant under conditions that were unusual. To each a messenger from God had announced the birth of her child. Each child would be very special, with a mission from God.

Even with these things in common it was evident that Mary's child would be the one who was unique. Elizabeth called Him her 'Lord'! Mary herself called Him her 'Saviour'!

Note verse 41: it was the Holy Spirit who gave Elizabeth the insight to comprehend that Mary's baby would be the Messiah. It is the Holy Spirit today who gives us the insight to embrace Mary's Son as our Saviour and Lord. These things are too much for our little minds to take in. A human baby—God! That is too much for us to believe. That is why (is it not?) God saw fit to make faith in His Son a gift (Ephesians 2:8). It is a gift from God and it is wrought in us by the operation of God's own Holy Spirit.

O thank You, God, for Your unspeakable gift (2 Corinthians 9:15).

NAMING THE BABY
Luke 1:57–65

Naming a baby can be a difficult task. Some parents look for a name that is particularly euphonious. Some use the initials of the parents. Some name a child after a relative or friend. Some research name meanings and use one that seems appropriate. Some choose Biblical names exclusively.

We don't get disturbed, however, about what our neighbors call their new baby! Even if they call him Hezekiah Hildebrand Hoffminster we don't make too much of a fuss. Maybe sometimes we should make a fuss in defense of the poor child who will be bearing this label all his life, but we don't.

Among the Jews of the first century A.D. the custom of naming a son after his father, or at least after someone in his family, was so prevalent that to give the name John to this boy caused quite a stir. The neighbors were up in arms. And their amazement was heightened when the announcement of the child's name caused the obedient father to regain his speech!

Why did God do this strange thing? And why did He put this account in the Bible? What does He have here for us?

Zacharias would have been a good name. It means 'Jehovah has remembered.' Is John any more appropriate? This name means 'Jehovah has been gracious.'

It is difficult to see any greater significance of the name John over Zacharias. It is more likely that God wanted to choose the name Himself to underline the fact that this child was very special to Him. It is certain that He was teaching Zacharias and Elizabeth a choice lesson in His interest and care.

It is not so vital today what we name our children. We do not expect God to give us a name in a supernatural way. What we can learn from Zacharias is complete acceptance of God's will! It was not, 'We have decided . . .' It was, 'His name is John!'

WHAT MANNER OF CHILD SHALL THIS BE?
Luke 1:66–80

With such unusual circumstances surrounding his birth, of course the neighbors wondered what kind of person this baby John would grow up to be! Zacharias, his tongue loosened, burst out in praise to God, prophesying in the power of the Holy Ghost. He blessed God and traced His revelation in the past through prophets of old. He told the infant boy he too would be a prophet, preparing the way for the Lord Himself.

The child grew. He became 'strong in spirit' (1:80). The Lord was with him. His promise to the parents would be kept through this child.

As we today look at an infant does not this same question come to our mind: 'What manner of child shall this be?' (1:66). We are anxious about his well-being and his personal equipment. We wonder about his vocation. But most important, will he be a prophet of God?

We cannot know. We have not had a messenger from God speak to us about this child. We do, however, have within our power the training of this child to equip him to learn of God. Let us recognize the possibility that he might become a prophet of God. And let us pray to that end!

IN BETHLEHEM
Luke 2:1–20

It was a busy time in the little town. Every Jew whose ancestors were from Bethlehem was returning to be taxed in this general taxation which the Roman Emperor had decreed. Joseph, like every other Jew of the time, had full knowledge of his family tree. He was well aware that he was of the line of David.

The women were taxed, too, and had to travel to the town of their fathers. Even pregnant women, under the rule of the ruthless Augustus, were forced to make the trip. Augustus considered himself autonomous. But he was an instrument in the hand of the Sovereign God to accomplish the fulfilment of the prophecy of Micah 5:2: 'But thou, Bethlehem Ephratah, though thou be little among the thousands of Judah, yet out of thee shall he come forth unto me that is to be ruler in Israel; whose goings forth have been from of old, from everlasting.'

God's ways are past finding out. He used the decree of a world monarch to accomplish His purpose! He used a full inn to bring about the birth of His Son in the most modest of surroundings. The baby was born exactly where and when

He chose. All circumstances were bent toward the accomplishment of His purpose. The humblest manger in a very ordinary stable. An unpretentious town. It was all part of the humiliation of the Son of God who left the riches of heaven to be born into the race of men. It was all part of the evidence of the love of the Sovereign God for sinners.

SACRIFICE FOR SIN
Luke 2:21–24

Jesus was fully man. He was in the likeness of sinful flesh (Romans 8:3). He was born of a woman, born under the law, sent to redeem them that were under the law (Galatians 4:4). He fulfilled all righteousness (Matthew 3:15) and performed all the obligations of the law. This is why He was circumcised.

The rules concerning circumcision and purification were reminders of the sin inherent in every child who is born. When a sacrifice was offered for Jesus, He, although Himself without sin, was placing Himself voluntarily under the law as part of His identification with the people whom He came to save.

Luke, the physician-historian, gives us the details of this event because of their larger significance. Mary was ceremonially unclean for forty days and her baby with her. Now it was the custom to bring to the temple a sacrifice for cleansing. So a lamb and a pigeon, or in cases of poverty two pigeons, were offered in place of the one who was sacrificing. This was symbolic of the acknowledgement of guilt before God: 'The wages of sin is death'! (Romans 6:23).

O God, thank You for sending Your Son and causing Him to be willing to take on the likeness of our sinful nature. Thank You for causing Him later to be a sacrifice for us Your people. Thank You for Your Book that makes it all so plain!

THE AWAITED STAR
Luke 2:25–35

How do we accept death as it comes to our home, whether it comes to a grandparent, a parent, or a child? Is there peace at such a time, undergirding us through the sorrow? Simeon said, 'Lord, now lettest thou thy servant depart in peace . . .' (2:29).

Geldenhuys pictures a slave in ancient Israel, on a lonely hill at night, keeping watch on behalf of his master for the rising of a particular star. After waiting long hours he finally sees the star rising, bright and beautiful. He announces it with joy. Then he is released from his charge and freed from further watch.

This is the picture of Simeon. Malachi had spoken of the coming of the 'Sun of righteousness' (Malachi 4:2). Simeon was waiting for this Sun, this Star of the House of Jacob. The Holy Spirit had revealed to him 'that he should not see death before he had seen the Lord's Christ' (2:26). Now he stands at last with the Christ-child in his arms! His task is completed. He may depart in peace.

Simeon's announcement is of a salvation which is to include all people. God had given indications of this through the years, and with ever-increasing clearness! The family of God is to be extended far beyond the walls of Jerusalem and the bounds of Palestine. The Star will project its healing rays to the ends of the earth and will enable God's people to have peace, even at the point of death.

The way we accept death is an indication of our relationship with the Saviour. Are we anticipating being with Him? Do we really believe that we shall be with Him? Are we confident that a departing believing loved one is now with the Saviour, which is 'far better' (Philippians 1:23)?

And during life are we making sure that we and the members of our family are aware of the importance of believing God's Word concerning the way of salvation?

ANNA THE WIDOW
Luke 2:36–38

What do widows do with their lives? The life of a woman, designed to be a helper, is very much bound up with the life of her husband. She usually depends upon him for protection and support, but she depends upon him more for love and companionship. Since the life expectancy of women is greater than that of men, the woman may well expect that she may outlive her spouse.* And when he is gone there is a deep void. What does she do?

If she is a Christian she will find that her Saviour can ease the ache. He can, during these years to come, mean more to her than ever before! This will not be automatic, but by God's grace it can occur. But how? Again we ask, what can a widow do?

What did Anna do? She spent her time actively serving God. In many cases widows have fewer responsibilities than other women. There are many things they can do in the form of service in God's kingdom. Now is the time to take a hard look at themselves and their gifts, perhaps even in consultation with their minister, and see how they may best serve God in this new period in their lives. There are persons who desperately need a friend or a home, lonely young people who need a foster aunt. Some widows express their love and concern for others by visiting, sending notes, taking flowers or cookies to shut-ins. Some volunteer their secretarial skills to the church. Some perform a real ministry with Christian books. Some take a special interest in other widows. And, most of all, many widows rejoice that they have time to study God's Word and pray as never before!

* According to the Statistical Abstract published in 1976, a female aged thirty in 1977 has a life expectancy of 78.2 years and a male 71.8 years.

When the husband dies life is not over for her! God has many special things for the woman who, like Anna, purposes to serve Him. There will be loneliness certainly, but if she belongs to God her life can even take on new dimensions during these years.

JESUS GOES TO CHURCH
Luke 2:39–52

The boy Jesus enjoyed church. This was not because the church had a good youth program or because it was the custom for everyone in Nazareth to attend. He enjoyed church because there He was able to attend to the business of His Father (2:49). He enjoyed church because this was His Father's house and He had a true and close relationship with His Father. He and His Father were ever and always one! 'I and my Father are one' (John 10:30).

But let us go on to verse 51. He was also subject to His human mother and father under the law. He, God come in the flesh, was submissive to His parents in the flesh! And His earthly parents took Him to church.

Our children should be shown the privilege of following in the footsteps of Jesus as they are submissive to their parents. They should be shown that as they go to church with their parents they are doing what Jesus did. Church attendance should be a normal event. There should not be a weekly decision as to whether to go. It should be, moreover, a cheerful occasion, not a chore. The attitude should not be, 'Do we *have* to go to church?' but rather 'We *look forward* to going to church!'

This is the place where God has planned that His children should gather together and engage in His business. David said, 'I was glad when they said unto me, Let us go into the house of the Lord' (Psalm 122:1).

Really, now, if Jesus attended church regularly, do we have an option?

A SON DEPARTS
Luke 15:1–13

One of the most difficult times in the life of parents is the time when their son or daughter leaves home. It is difficult when this is an actual geographic departing. The son (or daughter) may even take to the road, having no real plan or destination. He may move into an apartment by himself or into a house with friends. He may go away to college or into the military service. Or he may leave to get married. Whatever the case, this represents a breach in the close relationship which has been maintained between home and child through many years.

But the parent realizes, if he is a thinking person, that this breach is a part of life as God designed it. His son is growing up and becoming an independent human being. The parent adjusts to the departure and attempts to rearrange his life style.

The kind of departure that is most difficult to accept is the ideological, when the child departs from the way of thinking and living of his family. He may do this and not even leave home. But he is gone.

The amazing thing about the father in this parable is his attitude at such a time. He respects the decision of the departing son. He gives him what he asks for. Without rancor he says goodbye. His attitude at the departure leaves the way open for the return!

Jesus is telling us about the heavenly Father, but there is a lesson, too, for us in our own dealings with our family. How needful is this lesson for parents who have ahead of them this difficult experience of the departure of a son or daughter! We should pray for a gentle spirit, a calm understanding of the problems of our day. This young person has his whole life ahead of him. Sometimes he is given strength to follow God's way readily. Sometimes he cannot just follow in our way without exploring the alternatives. When he goes we do not know what to expect. We can do nothing else but let him go, being sure to leave the door ajar for his return!

A SON RETURNS
Luke 15:11–24

If it is difficult to see a young son leave, it is equally difficult sometimes to cope with his return. He will have changed. He will have grown taller and more independent. It will be difficult to reestablish a father-son relationship. He may *look* different and may have acquired new habits of which we disapprove. This is a tense moment, though we have prayed for it! How we need additional prayers to deal with it!

What did this father do? He went to meet his son. He sympathized with his experiences. He *physically* welcomed him, embracing and kissing him! He accepted the confession without a sermon. He fed and clothed him. He shared his joy openly with family and friends.

Note: he went to meet him before the son confessed his sin. He refrained from condemnation or lecture on this glad day. He did not try to obtain a financial accounting. He did not require the son to have a shower or a haircut before he would touch him. He did not hide his joy under a proud reserve or a wounded spirit. There is an openness that is touchingly portrayed in this brief story.

Lord, be with us as parents. Teach us how to let our child depart when he must. Teach us to wait prayerfully through the hours or the years. Teach us how to welcome him back!

[204]

If we fail at this point, it is possible he will go away again never to return.

THE OLDER BROTHER
Luke 15:25–32

Jesus told this story because the scribes and Pharisees had been critical of his friendliness with 'sinners' (15:2). They should have seen in it a portrayal of themselves as the older brother, resentful because the heavenly Father welcomed back the younger son who had been a prodigal.

The main thrust of this story is in this section, which often does not receive as much attention as it warrants. There should have been rejoicing in the heart of the older brother when his younger brother repentantly rejoined the family circle. The scribes and Pharisees should have been glad, as are the angels in heaven when a sinner repents. The Jews should have been glad when the gospel message was drawing Gentiles into the family of God. We conservative Christians should be glad to welcome 'sinners' and persons of different skin color, features, manners and habits into our fellowship in the house of God.

In the context of the home, each member should be able to forgive and forget when one member confesses his past sins and wants to take up his place in the home again.

Notice that the father pleaded with the older brother to join in the welcome. As the older

[205]

brother pouted and felt sorry for himself the father reminded him that through the years he had received favors and enjoyed the security of the home.

Jealousy, resentment, rivalry—our homes are marred by them. But they should not keep us from expressing our joy at the salvation of one member! 'This thy brother was dead, and is alive again; and was lost, and is found' (15:32). Unfeigned, spontaneous joy at the repentance of a prodigal is indeed a testimony to the validity of the Christian experience!

GUEST AT A WEDDING
John 2:1-11

Jesus was invited to the wedding at Cana. They wanted Him to be there to participate in the joyful celebration. They had confidence that He would find time in His busy schedule to rejoice with them on this happy day. Happy the couple who invite Jesus to their wedding and desire to have Him share their joy on that day of days!

Jesus accepted the invitation to the wedding at Cana. That made the difference between an embarrassing social fiasco and a joyous event with very special refreshments! Jesus came and participated in the activities, showing real empathy with the chagrined host when the supply of wine was gone. The One who Himself made the grapes now miraculously made wine without grapes!

Today we do not look for a miracle when we invite Jesus to our wedding, but in the broad sense of the word we do experience the wonderful and the extraordinary when He is a part of our plans. His presence can bring assurance that this marriage can be a lasting, growing relationship at a time when one of every two marriages ends in divorce! His presence itself is joy, a joy which the world cannot know.

Jesus adds a new dimension to the home. He daily changes water into 'wine that maketh glad the heart of man' (Psalm 104:15).

ADOPTION
John 8:31–59

Everyone is in a family. Even if the family is broken or all other members deceased, each person who ever lived belongs to some family tree.

In the spiritual realm everyone is in a family, too. Had there been no fall, all men of all periods of time would have been in the family of God. But since the fall mankind has been by nature of the family of Satan. 'Children of wrath' is the way the Apostle Paul describes them (Ephesians 2:3).

This is horrible to contemplate, yet it was a truth taught by the Lord himself: 'If God were your father, ye would love me . . . Ye are of your father the devil' (John 8:42,44).

Quickly we must remind ourselves that in His

grace God adopted a people for His family. Not only this, but He has made a promise to His people that includes their children in His plan.

Thank You, Father, for adopting us into Your family! Thank You for sending the only Son who was really Yours without need of adoption to die for us so that we, too, could be Your sons and daughters.

Some of us have adopted children into our family. Have we explained to them that we, also, are adopted? Do they see the grace and love of the heavenly Father who has adopted us and through whom this earthly family can be united in ties even stronger than blood?

THE FAMILY OF GOD
Acts 9:36–43

In John's Gospel we heard from the lips of the Lord Jesus about the family of God. Now we look into the period of the early church, after our Lord has died, risen, and ascended into heaven. What does God tell us in the Acts of the Apostles about His family? Indirectly He tells us about His family through the life of Dorcas.

Dorcas was probably a widow or unmarried. There is no evidence that she had any family responsibilities. But she was a member of the family of God and she shared herself, her goods, the fruit of her hands, her love, with other family members. No wonder they loved her!

In the providence of God we have in our churches women like Dorcas, who live alone, without families of their own, but members of the family of God. What is our relationship with them? Do we include them in the activities of the church and its fellowship? If they have a financial need, do we as the body of Christ help them meet it? If they have need of a lawyer, a carpenter, a doctor, an errand-boy, a counselor, a gardener, do we offer our services? Do we invite them to our homes for meals or visits? As fellow members of the family of God we should do these things quite spontaneously.

Could we adopt a widow as an aunt for our children? God has commanded us to care for widows and orphans—the alone ones. What reason do we have for being so casual in obeying His provision for social security?

And as for the woman alone, whether a widow or unmarried, she must be willing to communicate her need and to accept from her sisters and brothers in Christ what they offer as coming from God. This is God's way and all of us should rejoice in His concern for each one of His people.

COME TO MY HOUSE
Acts 16:1–15

Lydia, like the Shunammite woman, opened her home to the servant of God. What a blessing to Paul to be in such a Christian home! Only one who has been on the road really knows what it is to enjoy a home atmosphere along the way. And to Paul, whose journeys were fraught with danger and persecution, this was a real respite.

But don't you think that the home itself was the more blessed? To have the apostle Paul in your home! To hear him pray at the table and open the Scriptures to you and your family! To experience the compassion of his great heart and to feel his love! To bring your questions to him and hear his answers from the Scriptures and from his vast store of knowledge of God's truth! What a blessing!

When was the last time you gave yourself and your family the privilege of the presence of one of God's special servants in your home? Have you ever sat spellbound at your own table while a missionary from overseas told experiences of God's care in the face of danger and illness? Have you ever rejoiced over the account of the growth of new churches God is using His servants to raise up in our own land? Have you ever sat at your own table with your own pastor and come to see in a refreshing way some of the truths you have really been wanting to explore with someone trained to explain them more fully?

And are you aware of the presence of the Lord Jesus Himself in your home? There is an old plaque which speaks of Jesus as 'the unseen guest at every meal.' Lord, grant that we may more fully realize that You dwell in our home.

AND YOUR HOUSEHOLD
Acts 16:16–34

Despite the placing of these prisoners in maximum security, they were escaping. The jailor was grasping his sword to take his own life rather than submit to execution for failure to fulfil his duty. But the prisoners assured him that they were not running away, so he must not take his life.

This jailor had seen enough of Paul and Silas to believe that they had something he needed. 'What must I do to be saved?' he asked them. He was given the message that would bring salvation not only for time but for eternity.

He brought Paul and Silas into his home, and he and all in his house listened to the gospel story. 'He was baptized, he and all his household' (16:33). He 'set food before them, and rejoiced greatly, having believed in God with his whole household' (16:34 NASB).

This section has been bandied about by Christians. Some assume from it that each member believed, so was entitled to baptism because of his personal faith. Some claim that it sets forth the right of the children of believers to baptism because of the covenant which God had made with Abraham to be a God to His people and to their children.

With no information concerning the ages of the members of the household we would not use this incident by itself to substantiate infant baptism. But it is one of several instances of household baptism. And it is consonant with God's dealing with men through the ages. He has worked in families in the past and He does so today! He includes our families in the covenant. Our young children enjoy the fellowship of God and His larger family. They experience the love and concern as well as the training and discipline of the church.

In the Old Testament, the sign of the covenant was circumcision, and male children were entitled to it. In the New Testament the sign is changed. Now it does not involve the shedding of blood. The Supreme Sacrifice has been made! Now it involves water, which is used in Scripture to typify cleansing by the Holy Spirit. Children of believers today are not less favored by God. They are included in His covenant and have a right to baptism, the outward sign of this inclusion. And now, in keeping with the enlarged privileges of the New Testament era, the covenant sign is one adapted to little girls as well as boys.

The whole family of the Philippian jailor rejoiced! Not only had God spared the father's life, He had provided eternal life for the father and all the household as well.

WE ARE ALSO GOD'S OFFSPRING
Acts 17:22–34

From Greek poetry comes the line, 'We are also his offspring' (17:28). By now Athens was emerging to some extent from its polytheism despite the presence still of many statues and altars to gods and goddesses. Zeus was gaining supremacy among the gods and was being regarded as creator and ruler.

This god, the poets had said, was father of men. In the Greek religion and mythology there had been intermarriage between gods and human beings on numerous occasions. So it was an easy transition to regard Zeus as father of men as well as their creator. If we who are persons are the children of Deity then we ought not to think that the 'Godhead' is like gold or silver or stone, an image formed by the art and imagination of man. Thus Paul reasons.

As we look into the wonder of personality we have a small inkling of the nature of God, in whose image man was created. True, this sin-marred creature shows little resemblance to his Father Creator! But men redeemed by God's only-begotten Son increasingly partake again of the divine nature by the influences of His indwelling Spirit.

For all their wisdom, what an inadequate view of man and God the Greeks had! The simplest Christian believer understands far more than they. Never need we or our children in secular schools apologize for our faith. We are wiser than the remarkable Greeks. We have more understanding than all our teachers (Psalm 119:99). We are the offspring of Jehovah, the Creator-God. He made us and, further, He has adopted us into His special family.

GOD GAVE THEM UP
Romans 1

In order to understand our child and his need for discipline we must understand the nature of man. We must understand what it means that he is born in sin. Then we must see how sin progressively masters a man. A man does not remain on a plateau from birth to death, nor is there an evolution of his moral character. The normal course of a man is that of decline.

Romans 1 is the classic section of Scripture to point this out. We read here about God's revelation to man and man's persistent refusal to recognize it. We see how 'God gave them over in the sinful desires of their heart to sexual impurity' (1:24 NIV). We see again that 'God gave them over to shameful lusts' (1:26 NIV). And finally 'He gave them over to a depraved mind' (1:28 NIV). Downward, downward, downward!

Does our experience substantiate this? It most surely does. Today we tell a 'white lie.' Tomorrow it will be easier to tell a more substantial one. In fact, it may appear necessary to tell several to cover up the first. How well it has been said:

> O, what a tangled web we weave
> When first we practise to deceive.*

* Sir Walter Scott: *Marmion* Canto vi, 17.

But it is really more than this. When God is rebuffed repeatedly, when, in the face of overwhelming evidence of the existence of His love and demands, a person keeps saying 'No' to Him, it is as though God replies, 'All right, go your own way. In My common grace I have been granting you some ability to live a moral life and to enjoy the world and the people I have made, but since you fail to acknowledge Me and be thankful, I will take My hands off you. You will be left to yourself!'

If, however, a man turns to Christ, his life is redirected. Sometimes he may slip. Nevertheless, slowly but surely he proceeds to go upward in his walk. God teaches, helps, chastises, lovingly and faithfully taking His child by the hand and drawing him upward, upward, upward.

This we need to have firmly in mind in order to discipline our child intelligently from the earliest days. Our training has to be rigorous in order to combat the downward pull of sin! The way of salvation has to be set clearly before him, that his course may be changed!

We rejoice in the love and patience of our God to draw the recalcitrant to Himself. This love and patience we see in His dealings with believers, too, as He draws us up toward the place He has prepared for us. He would have us to be like Him and He will accomplish this transformation fully one day when we are brought face to face with our Saviour.

INNOCENT BABE
Romans 3:9–24

When a child is born into the world he *seems* so innocent and so pure. It is not difficult, really, to think of him as a *tabula rasa,* a clean slate, whose environment will imprint upon him the evil that becomes by manhood such a part of his life.

It is here that many of us get on the wrong track as parents. We fail to see the need of training the child when he is such a tiny baby. We readily recognize that he needs love and it is very easy to give him this because he is so lovable. But it is more difficult to recognize his need of discipline and training and give it to him. Indeed, the need for discipline in the infant is difficult to discern unless we are aware that the innocence we are assuming is only apparent!

It is important for us to study Romans 3 along with Romans 1 to learn what God says about the nature of man. The inherently sinful nature of man may be very ugly and depressing for us who are parents to contemplate. But it is the truth of God and we need to be reminded of it that our backbones might be stiffened! This chapter should impress upon us the need gently to train, instruct and correct from the earliest days. Beginning with the simple lesson that beds are made for sleeping and that mother knows that her baby needs sleep, the training should proceed. The proud, self-assertive spirit of the baby needs gradually but surely to come to rest in the wisdom of those parents to whose care God has intrusted him.

Romans 3 should also impress upon us the need to communicate as the years proceed the liberating gospel of God both by our example and our precept.

LOVING THE UNLOVELY
Romans 5:1–10

The Greek word *agape* is assuming a prominent place in the vocabulary of the Christian. And indeed it should, since it is so much in evidence in Scripture.

One aspect of this *agape* love is beautifully brought out in verses 6, 8 and 10 here. *Agape* love is integral with the lover and is based upon his character. It is not something that the beloved calls forth by his lovableness. When 'we were *yet sinners* Christ died for us!' (5:8).

Translated into the parent-child relationship this means that even the least lovely child must be loved by the parent. Parental love is not called forth merely by the winsomeness of the child. It is poured out of the heart of the parent who is empowered by God to love each child in a special way. Often this same unlovely child as he becomes more and more aware of the value of his soul in the sight of loving parents and of

God will, like the desert, 'blossom as the rose' (Isaiah 35:1).

With a heart of love a parent can see, especially if God has touched his eyes, talents and good characteristics of his child which are not apparent to others. Little realized potentials are recognized. It is the wise and loving parent who is able to encourage the child and help him strengthen what needs to be strengthened as well as weed out that which would choke the good plants.

We are everlastingly thankful to God for loving us while we were yet sinners! Let us pray that we may be enabled so to love our children.

MARRIED TO GOD
Romans 7

Paul uses the figure of marriage to help us understand our relationship to the law. Marriage is for life. 'The married woman is bound by law to her husband while he is living' (7:2 NASB). Any extramarital relationship makes the offender an adulterer. If, however, one partner dies, the other is freed from the marriage and may take another partner.

In the context of this discourse on sanctification Paul is showing us that when we are married to the law we are under the dominion of the law. The law is our husband and we are subject to it. Only death can sever this relationship to the law. We who are Christ's 'are become dead to the law by the body of Christ' (7:4). We are joined to God that we might bear fruit to God!

We read of the fruit of the womb. We are the wife. Our Lord is the husband. What is the fruit? In this allegorical sense we do not find the fruit applied to human beings in Scripture. So what does it mean? In Scripture the fruit represents the good works that God enables us to produce, the fruit of the Spirit, His Spirit!

Married to the Lord! Bearing fruit to God! Again the figure, and again the challenge to be faithful to the divine Husband and truly to bear fruit to His glory!

JOINT-HEIRS WITH CHRIST
Romans 8:14–28

The concept of all Christian wives being heirs with their Christian husbands 'of the gracious gift of life' (I Peter 3:7 NIV) is a precious one to us in our marriage. But here is a concept that further staggers us—'joint-heirs with Christ' (8:17). This takes the precious relationship of marriage and elevates it beyond our ability to contemplate!

God's Spirit dwelling within us gives us the assurance that we are indeed children of God. He enables us to cry out, Abba, Father (8:15). We have been adopted by the Sovereign God, being made His sons and daughters.

Jesus Christ is called also in the Scripture the Son of God! However, He is the Son by the very nature of things. Being God Himself, He is uniquely the Son. He alone is the only-begotten One.

As we look at these two great facts—our sonship and Christ's Sonship—we see clearly that we are brothers with Christ, co-heirs (NIV) with Him. As his fellows, we suffer with Him; as co-heirs we shall share in His glory (Romans 8:17).

Our hope in the midst of the sorrows and frailties of this life is the redemption of the body. Along with all creation, we shall be freed completely from the curse of sin that came upon man and all creation at the fall. Through Christ we are even now able to see victory over sin. But one day we shall be publicly recognized as the sons of God. Our adoption will be consummated and, together with our Co-heir, we shall come into our eternal heritage. That will be glory!

DELEGATED AUTHORITY
Romans 13:1–10

It is obvious that God expects church leaders to enhance their authority by ruling well, as Timothy admonished the elders (I Timothy 3:5). Ruling well in the home is a criterion of our ability to rule well elsewhere.

But as parents we do not possess authority basically because we have *earned* it. Our authority has been established by God. It is *delegated.*

God is a God of order, hating confusion and anarchy. No one knows as He does the state of man's heart. He is aware of the incipient rebellion in the spirit of a fallen man, even when that man has been redeemed. So he has set up a framework in which men are to operate. He has set up authority. That is why even the worst of governments is to be respected since it is better than no government at all!

There is such a thing, also, as *usurped* authority, or self-delegated authority. The woman who decides that her husband is not going to rule over her, or the child who resists his parents' control, is like the person in Romans 13:2 who resists authority in a civil government and, like this person, the woman or child is opposing the ordinance of God.

God's perfect plan, woven into the warp and woof of creation and human history, may not be circumvented. We are to 'render to all their dues' (13:7). This is 'for good' in the state, in the church, and in the home (13:4).

Husband and father, God has made you to exercise authority. Do you wield this authority in accordance with His law of love? Do you rule in awe, remembering it is only because God delegated authority to you that you have a right to it?

ACCEPTANCE
Romans 14:1–13

We must accept ourselves. We must accept one another. Parents must accept their children. This word *accept* is much used today, but we ought not to think it is a new concept. The Apostle Paul says, 'Now accept the one who is weak in faith' (14:1 NASB); 'Accept one another, just as Christ also accepted us to the glory of God' (Romans 15:7 NASB). He is telling us to treat people, even weak people, with dignity, as having been made in the image of God and as having been accepted by God as they come to Him through His Son, 'accepted in the beloved' (Ephesians 1:6).

Are we distressed by the life style which our children have adopted? How careful we must be not to reject our children because of this. We must look behind the exterior and accept the person. Behavior and even opinions are not inseparable from the person himself. To accept a person is not necessarily to condone his behavior or speech. The Lord Jesus ate with sinners. The worst of men can be transformed by the power of God.

We must allow for differences of opinion on many matters within the church and within the home as well. Not one of us is completely sanctified! All our opinions have constantly to be held up to scrutiny in the light of God's truth. There are many areas in which the clear-cut rights and wrongs of Scripture are difficult for us to apply in the complex situations of life. Let us as parents not be so proud intellectually or spiritually that we regard our private applications of the principles of Scripture as absolute. Thus, 'Accept the one who is weak in the faith' sometimes means to accept our children—and their friends!

You have accepted us, dear Father; grant that we may accept one another!

FAMILY TIES
Romans 16:1–6

At first glance this section may have seemed an unlikely source for devotional meditation. But it calls to mind two subjects that are appropriate for us to consider: that all members of the family of God have a vital function; and that the family of God has reached a new significance since Calvary.

In our zeal to preserve God's order for society we sometimes underestimate the place He has given to women in His family, the church. They do not, as the conservative Christian holds, have official teaching positions. They are not elders, either teaching or ruling elders. But we see here in Scripture that God did use them to assist the apostles, not only in the kitchen and sewing-room but in the handling of God's Word and in dealing with people. They were an integral part of the body of Christ, using their many gifts where they are appropriate. And so it is today.

Here the readers in Rome (and this surely included men!) were instructed to *assist* Phoebe in any business in which she might have a need of their help! Priscilla and Aquila are said to have been helpers who 'laid down their own necks' for Paul's life (16:4). Women figure largely among those who are greeted. There is no discrimination on the basis of sex in the family of God.

In Old Testament times, except for a few strangers who were welcomed, the 'faithful' were of one blood. They were a family as children of their Covenant God and a family as children of Abraham as well. There was a bond of fellowship that bound them doubly.

Today, and we see this in our reading in Romans, even though the bond is not biological, even though the 'faithful' are drawn from Jew and Gentile, black and white, rich and poor, there is a bond which is even stronger still than that in the Old Testament. The biological family is just as important in God's eyes as it was in any time of history, but with the emergence of the cross-family fellowship of the body of Christ we see a new phenomenon such as the Old Testament writers do not give us. And Christians can never be content until all their natural families are embraced in the spiritual or *supernatural* family.

This chapter becomes more precious as we see in it the functions of each member of the family and as we see also the place of the family of God in society. O God, we thank You that all of Your Word is profitable to us.

CHURCH DISCIPLINE
1 Corinthians 5:1–13

How many churches today actually deal with sin in their membership? We in the church are soft, softer than God! A little leaven leavens the whole lump. God wants the sin out of His church just as He wanted the leaven taken from the bread of the Passover. This chapter should be studied by the governing bodies of our churches and applied—to the glory of God—that the family of God may be purified.

Within the church at Corinth there was a case of incest. Paul tells the church to remove the guilty party from the body, to cut him off from the fellowship in order that he might realize the precariousness of his spiritual condition and hopefully seek God's forgiveness and be restored.

The failure to administer discipline in the church today is without doubt one of the reasons that the church is weak. The church should be teaching the law of God. This teaching is not just via sermons! Part of the teaching requires dealing with infringements of God's law! Where this is neglected offenders will not be brought face to face with their sin and the rest of the body will not be able to profit by the failures of their brothers and take warning concerning the seriousness of sinning against God's law.

[225]

In our families we have seen how important discipline is. Christians should be stressing this as no others do. How, then, can we suppose that God the Father is indifferent to discipline in His family the church?

SINS AGAINST OUR BODY
1 Corinthians 6:12–20

There was a day when sex outside marriage was considered the grossest of sins. It was in a place by itself, the only sin for which a young woman was singled out with a scarlet 'A' which she would have to wear embroidered on her clothing until the day of her death! What has happened today? Have we come to gloss over sexual sins? Or have we come to understand that these sins are not alone to be considered gross, but that hate and envy and materialism are gross, too? At any rate, we can more readily accept the person who lapses into sexual sin but who truly repents, than could our New England forebears. Jesus by His example teaches we must accept such an one.

However, let us not lose sight of the force of verse 18. Very clearly it states that sexual sins are sins against our own bodies. Our bodies are the temple of the Holy Spirit. We do not own them. They were made by God and they have been bought back by God at the price of the death of His own Son. The fact that we recognize the gravity of other sins does not mean that we

[226]

can minimize in our thinking the gravity of this particular kind of sin.

We sin against our bodies in ways other than by illicit sex. Neglect of health can be sin, whether by failure to get medical care, or by failure to get sufficient rest or a proper diet or sufficient exercise. The use of tobacco, alcohol, or drugs which weakens the body or our control of it, surely does not honor our Creator. In many ways we sin against our bodies.

Who is not guilty of disrespect to the temple of the Holy Spirit? What a gracious God we have who does forgive *all* the sins of his people, even those against our own bodies, as we come to Him, confessing our sins, in our Saviour's name.

MARITAL RESPONSIBILITY
1 Corinthians 7:1–7

The church at Corinth was having problems with sex. All around was promiscuity. In the midst of that there was a reaction. Some either did not marry at all or else refrained from sex within marriage. The people had written to Paul for advice. What was his response?

First Paul speaks to the single person, assuring him that it is quite right to choose not to marry. It is good, fine, commendable. But he warns him that, in the face of the immorality and temptation on every side, marriage, monogamous marriage, is generally preferable to remaining single. Man has a need which God implanted and which God designed should be met within marriage.

Then Paul speaks to married couples. He warns that they, too, must be aware of the problems and temptations around them. They must not turn ascetic, but realize the plan of God for mankind, and find their joy and fulfilment in each other, not fearing to give themselves to each other freely. He suggests that an exception may be made when they agree to set aside a special period for prayer, in order that marriage may not hinder the maintenance of their own personal relationship with God. But the general rule should be that there is freedom for the exercise of their conjugal rights.

Paul goes on in the sixth verse to clarify his original statement concerning marriage. He wants to be sure that the Corinthians do not interpret his words as a command to marry. Rather, they have the right, they are *permitted* to marry. It is just that they do not *have* to exercise that right. He, as a single person who was free to travel for the Lord and whose absence or whose persecution would not cause hardship to a wife or children, was of the opinion that the single state has a real advantage during dangerous days in the history of the church. The Lord had given him, furthermore, the special gift of continence, and this was for the furtherance of the gospel.

These verses are often held up to scorn and are presented as evidence that Paul had a low estimate of marriage. But is it not clear in the context of the writing that this is not the case?

[228]

Recall, too, the high view of marriage which Paul sets forth in Ephesians 5! Indeed, it was *because* Paul had this high view of marriage that he warned against marrying lightly, without the ability to maintain the relationship in the responsible way that God designed. This warning is for Americans as well as Corinthians.

THE SINGLE PERSON
1 Corinthians 7:7–9

Paul continues his discussion on marriage. He is saying in verse 7 that the ability to remain single without undue sexual struggle is a special gift he has received of God. He would like—he speaks in hyperbole—to see *everyone* have this gift so that the gospel ministry could go forth unhampered by the cares of families! This extreme statement reminds us of Paul's other declaration (called forth also by his zeal for the gospel ministry) that he could wish himself 'accursed' for the sake of his brethren the Jews (Romans 9:3).

When a person loses his partner Paul suggests that it might be best for him or her to remain unmarried. But if a strong sexual urge is a problem, Paul says it is better to re-marry. Paul presents the arguments that Jesus used, that lust is really adultery, so that a person who finds himself unable to cope with his desires surely should marry. Despite the restriction marriage may place

[229]

on the work of the gospel, it is preferable to being single and having an adulterous heart!

Those of us who are married sometimes have to be reminded in the midst of our enthusiasm for the married state that there are some for whom God has planned a life of service for Himself that can be better achieved as a single person. There is room in the church for all sorts of gifts. Let us not plan our activities and groups in such a way that those who are single will feel that they are being considered as some strange breed! And let us try to conquer this attitude that everyone ought to marry! Let us recognize the existence of the gift of continence in the church today. It *is* a gift, of course, and not a thing that a church can impose on any individual. It is a personal gift of God as much tailored to the individual as the gift of teaching or any other gift!

O for the ability to discern these things in our own lives and the lives of others!

DIVORCE
1 Corinthians 7:10–16

Paul turns to the married again, this time warning the Christian person against divorce. If a person has divorced his spouse he should either be reconciled to his former partner or else refrain from remarrying. Here Paul is presenting what the Lord Jesus had taught during His earthly life. Jesus has *commanded* married people to stay together. This is not simply 'good' (to use Paul's term in verse 1): it is a requirement of God. Marriage is a permanent contract and sexual relations with others outside that union are adulterous.

In verse 12 Paul turns to those in mixed marriages ('the rest,' he calls them) and gives special details over and above what had been spoken by Christ during His ministry. Paul says that if a Christian man has an unbelieving partner who is content to live with him, he is not to initiate a divorce. For, he argues, the believing partner has a sanctifying influence over the unbeliever, and the Lord in His grace may even use the Christian man to bring his wife to salvation! Furthermore, children of such a marriage are 'holy' in that they are granted the protecting arm of the church and come under Christian influences in the home, such as godly teaching and the prayers of a loving parent to a Covenant God.

However, if there is not peace in the home and the unbelieving partner does proceed toward a divorce, the believer should not contest it but allow it to proceed. The believer is not under bondage to an unbeliever in such a case. If he were, he would have to renounce his faith in order to keep the marriage. For in this instance the unbeliever's departure is tantamount to rejection of the Christian faith. Let him (or her) be gone, Paul is saying. The believer is not to keep on fighting against this divorce by bringing up the argument that his (or her) testimony might still win the mate! It is important in the sight of God that we live in an atmosphere of peace. To this He has called us, not to the bondage that requires either renunciation of our faith or constant strife.

How very practical are these verses in our day! Does this help us to see God's will in our own home? Does it help us in counselling someone else?

MORE WORDS TO THE UNMARRIED
1 Corinthians 7:24–35

As Paul continues in verse 25 he turns again to the single person. He reminds the Corinthians of the distress in which people were living at the time of his writing, and expresses his conviction that, to escape such distress, a young woman might well remain unmarried. This follows what he has been saying in verses 20 to 24.

This is the burden of verses 27 and 28, also. In whatever state you are, Paul advises, remain that way. To be married will be an extra burden. Of course it is not sinful to marry, but the extra involvements with the things of this world which necessarily come along with marriage will have a tendency to hinder the Christian in his performance of the work of the Lord.

We who are married and have children know how true this is. Often it seems that our days are so completely filled with the absolute necessities involved in the care of a family that our time with God is neglected. Paul is a realist. He sees these difficulties and so he writes to the Corinthians in this vein. We are not to shed our marriage and its responsibilities! On the other hand there may be occasions when to remain unmarried is God's will for the individual.

Do you think this is all very impractical in the 1980's? Do you think it is merely interesting historically but not pertinent to us? Well, maybe that is true in our country today, but the day may be coming when we, also, will have distressing times such as the Corinthians had. Surely in some parts of the world this is true today. Remember, too, that it is necessary to understand the background of these matters so that when Paul or other Bible writers are attacked because of their views, we may be able to give an explanation of their rationale and point the sceptic to God's all-embracing plan and purpose for His creation.

FATHER OF THE BRIDE
1 Corinthians 7:36–40

Paul is careful not to omit anyone. Now he speaks to the father of a young girl of marriageable age who is still single. It is obvious that he is speaking of a time remote from ours when he says that a parent *may permit* his daughter to marry, if that seems the best thing to do! But if the parent has the strength to resist the pull and feels convinced that this is proper, he should *not permit* her mar-

[233]

riage! Paul is saying that in this 'present distress' it is better not to let one's daughter become involved in a marriage which might well be steeped in misery.

Should Christian parents be reassessing their looseness in marriage counselling in the home? Should the reins be tightened? Surely such matters need serious thought in the light of God's Word.

In verse 39 Paul goes over the material we discussed when Romans was before us. While a man and his wife are both alive, the one remains bound by law to the other. But if one of them dies the other is free to marry whomsoever he or she pleases, *"ONLY IN THE LORD"* (7:39).

Then we find a postscript: the wife—he specially mentions her—would be happier if she did not marry again, according to Paul's judgment, in which he feels the Spirit of God is directing him. The use of the term *happier* here meshes with the use of the word *good* in verse 1. It embraces all that has been said about the *goodness* of marriage, the giving by God of special gifts of chastity, the advantages of the single life as conferring more freedom to serve God. If ever verses have to be considered in context, these surely do!

As we conclude this portion one thing especially is borne in upon us. God is very much concerned about all aspects of our lives. Whether we marry and whom we marry is of supreme importance to Him. How we conduct ourselves generally with our spouse and how we act when the pressures build up are His concern. Let us submit our marriage to the scrutiny of His eye. He can make it a thing of beauty, a true reflection of Christ's marriage to His church!

HAIR STYLES
1 Corinthians 11:1–16

In this Greek 1st-century culture men did not cover their heads. Here, as generally throughout the world, their hair was shorter than was the hair of women. Women, on the other hand, not only wore their hair longer but either covered it with a veil or caught it neatly with a cord or net in a veil-like style. These were the customs that prevailed in the Corinth to which Paul wrote.

However, at gatherings for prayer or 'prophesying' (according to the gifts given to the church before the New Testament writings were available) there had grown up an abuse. It appears that the women, delighting in a liberation from the Greek social structure in which they had been subjugated, wished to express an equality with men. So when they participated during such gatherings they cast off their veils or veil-like hairdos. They had been restored by Christianity to a position of honor. Now they were abusing it and trying to be like men!

Paul is saying here that man, created with dominion over the creatures and headship over his wife, is the crown of creation and should not have his head covered. Christ is the head of the man. For a man to have his head covered would be to act like a woman.

On the other hand, it is appropriate that woman, who was designed to be man's helper, made after the likeness of man and for the glory of man, should have her head covered, either with a veil or long hair gathered up in a neat coiffure. For her to do otherwise would be offensive in a culture so oriented. To have her head uncovered would be to act like a man. It would be degrading to a woman. Probably prostitutes had their hair cropped and to have short hair would appear to place a woman among them.

Does this word of Paul have any bearing on our contemporary culture? This section is not detailed enough for us to understand all of the implications and it would be difficult to draw from it specific hard and fast rules for Christian men or women today. It seems to say to us, however, that God is pleased to have us accord with the customs appropriate for our sex within our own framework. To run counter to the established culture is to jeopardize our Christian testimony. This is not to say that we should blindly follow customs rooted in paganism. But our liberty should not cause us—as it caused the Corinthian women—defiantly or proudly to assert ourselves in ways that would harm our testimony for the One who has set us free!

LOVE, THE GREATEST GIFT
1 Corinthians 13

The word *love* has been largely stripped of its meaning. It has become synonymous with concepts as diverse as sex or benevolence or lack of hostility. So it is good to read 1 Corinthians 13 often and to sharpen our understanding of love in its most profound sense. Living, as we do, in an atmosphere of such weakened concepts, it is indeed necessary actually to reconstruct our own understanding of the meaning of *love* as well as of other words. Let us delve into its wealth as Scripture uses it to describe God's relationship toward His people and the relationship He would have us sustain toward Him and toward one another.

The contemporary Christian public has been made familiar with the three words for *love* available to the Greeks: *phileo, eros* and *agape. Phileo* means to have a benevolent feeling, a feeling of goodwill. We meet it in the word Philadelphia, which means 'brotherly love.' *Eros* refers to sexual love and we recognize it in our word erotic. *Agape* is the deeper, stronger word which Christian writers found best suitable to take over and adapt to their own use.

Agape is the word which is used most commonly in the New Testament. It refers to God's love for His people, their love for Him, and their love for one another. From its usage we understand how our God regards us and how He enables us to regard one another.

Masumi Toyotome speaks of three kinds of love from a different perspective.* First there is the "if" kind of love, which is given provided the recipient measures up to certain standards. Then there is the "because" kind of love, which is given as a result of what its object has done or looks like, or how its object makes the lover feel. And third, there is the "in spite of" love! This is the love which issues from a heart because of the nature of that heart, the love that is poured out, not *if* it is deserved, or *because* it is deserved. This is the love which the one who knows he is an unlovely sinner longs for!

This is the love of God the Father! Let us pray that He will in His grace channel this love through us to our spouse and to our children and to all the world around! This is the love of 1 Corinthians 13.

HOMES ARE FOR LEARNING
1 Corinthians 14:26–36

This passage is a key to church life. It is part of a section on gifts. In a way it is a parenthesis growing out of a section on the abuse of the charismatic gifts which had been plaguing Corinth. Paul found it necessary to remind the Cor-

* Toyotome, Masumi. *Three kinds of love.* Inter-Varsity Press, 1970.

inthians that those gifts were not to be a source of confusion, marring the order and peace of a congregation of His people.

At first reading (and even the fifty-first perhaps) this section might be very jarring to the ear of the woman who has been told she has 'come a long way.' The thought of being barred from speaking up and even asking questions at church may humiliate or even infuriate her! Even when presented with the argument that Paul is safe-guarding the calm and order of the body of Christ by what may or may not be a permanent regula-tion, and which may not apply equally in formal worship services and informal meetings, she may find her pride wounded.

But if we look at this passage (especially verse 35) in the larger context of the whole Bible we see that the apostle is assuming that *homes* are for learning! We stress at this point the impor-tance of the family of God, the communion of the saints, the body of Christ. And well we might! The church is the beloved bride of the Saviour. But as we look at the whole of God's revelation, we see that the *home,* instituted along with Adam and Eve, is the basic unit of society. It is the home primarily where God's Word is to be taught and lived.

So one of the most pertinent applications we can make of verse 35 may come as a surprise. As the God-ordained teacher in the home, the husband should see to it that he is able to answer the questions of an intelligent twentieth-century wife as well as those of his young children! As a prophet he is to speak forth God's truths with the authority of Scripture and through the Holy Spirit. If the home is for learning, the father is for teaching. Mother will normally teach the children much of the time, but the head of the Department of Bible is the father. If this is true, and if father takes his task seriously, the wife will feel free to ask questions of him and will find real security and satisfaction in his ability to fill his role!

UNEQUAL YOKES
2 Corinthians 6:11–18 and 7:1

Verse 14 of chapter 6 is frequently used to warn young people against marrying outside the faith. As we place it beside other verses of Scripture and the general tenor of God's Word, we see that it is in harmony with a universal teaching against mixed marriages.

If we are going to be honest in our use of Scripture, however, we should be aware that this is not the primary purpose of this particular verse. As we examine the verse in context we see that it has a broader application. This is a plea for separateness from the evil of this world. It is a warning to separate ourselves from unbelief, especially in our fellowship, our communion, our worship. It is chiefly a warning against involvement in situations and organizations in which men are gathered together in a professed worship and service of God.

Jesus ate with sinners and publicans. He is not asking us to build a wall between ourselves and unbelievers. We are the salt of the earth and men must be able to savor us freely. But we are not to enter into a formal connection with unbelievers in a religious context!

The church world in our day needs to re-read these verses. Let not the church hand them freely and carelessly to its young people contemplating marriage and then fail to take this context into consideration in its own affairs! May not our looseness in applying this principle in ecclesiastical affiliations have a bearing on the looseness of our children in applying it to their own marital choice?

NEITHER MALE NOR FEMALE
Galatians 3:15–29

What a full portion of revelation! It may seem inappropriate to focus on four selected words in this passage, but in our day there is need for these words to be stressed in order to answer some criticisms of the Scripture, and especially of Paul's epistles. The words in question read, 'neither male nor female' (3:28).

Conservative Christians differentiate between the functions of men and women in the divine economy. They feel that it is important to stress the fact that God would have men take the leadership in the family as well as in the family of God,

[241]

the home as well as the church. They likewise show from Scripture the need of the wife to be a submissive follower.

These teachings are incorrectly interpreted by certain church leaders who tell us that they mean the woman is a second-class Christian. So it is important to give attention to these words of Paul—'neither male nor female'—and to ascertain what he is actually saying.

Paul is here stressing that there is neither Jew nor Gentile in the sight of God. All believers, not just the chosen people of Old Testament days, are children of God. All are united in Christ and have been clothed in Christ's righteousness. To emphasize the all-inclusiveness of this coverage and the oneness of believers in Christ, he adds that there is neither bond nor free, 'there is neither male nor female.' Paul would include every category of the human family in his coverage without making any distinctions.

Believing husbands and wives are alike children of God. In His eye there is no difference. The differences we speak of are social and natural differences and apply in this world only! The woman who thoroughly grasps this and is aware of her standing with God will not fret at any temporal, positional difference between herself and her husband. She will be satisfied with what God has made her and will rest in His wisdom in doing all things well!

SPEAKING THE TRUTH IN LOVE
Ephesians 4:13–24

If we were to give in a sentence one of the most valuable secrets of success in inter-personal relations, that sentence might well be drawn from verse 15: *speak the truth in love.* Honest, loving communication promotes a good relationship. We have said it before. We say it again. Speaking the truth in love means, first of all, *speaking!* It means expressing those hidden feelings which may have been simmering within for years. There is no place for clamming up or applying the silent treatment. Speak!

Speaking the truth in love means speaking *truly.* We must not allow deceit or subterfuge to creep into the words we say. We must not gloss over our own sins or present a slanted viewpoint of a story or situation. Bring things out in utter honesty.

God's way does not resemble a group therapy approach which in some situations permits attacking others to give release to one's own built-up anger. There must be gentleness, an awareness of how the truth may really hurt the hearer or strain the relationship for a while. It requires speaking the truth *in love.* A loving presentation of the truth firmly and tenderly builds the desired relationship and promotes the growth of each believer.

Are there things in our marriage which have

been hidden, maybe for years, lying under the surface, smoldering, causing tension? Are there things which, tomorrow, when they can no longer be stifled, may result in an explosion capable of bringing injury to several persons? Now is the time to learn the lesson of Ephesians 4 and speak out concerning these things in all truth and in love.

There may be some hurt at first. But the surgeon hurts, too. After an initial adjustment the love will heal the hurt and there will be growth, both in the life of the speaker and in that of the one to whom he has spoken.

Be careful! Speaking the truth in love has the potential for harm! It takes a courageous and mature person to do it and a humble and mature person to accept it! However, we are still spiritually immature if we avoid it, and we are being disobedient to God!

GOD'S DEAR CHILDREN
Ephesians 5:1–20

Believers are God's children. This we have read all through Scripture. Here Paul calls us God's *'dear children'* (5:1). What an appellation for sinful creatures! What a responsibility it places upon us! So Paul tells us here how 'as dear children' we must 'walk' in order to be followers of God in deed.

We are to 'walk in love' (5:2). Our language is to be loving, never soiled by innuendos or distorted sex conversation or inappropriate levity concerning sacred things. Our communication is to be different from that of the world and people are to be able to tell the difference. Our conversation is to be characterized by thanksgiving to God.

We are not only *dear children*. We are *children of light*. Not only are we to have no fellowship with children of darkness, we are to reprove them. Not only are we to refrain from choosing our intimate companions from among those who take God's name in vain—we are to rebuke those who do! A life lived for God is a silent rebuke, too. If our *lives* are not a reproof, surely our *words* cannot be.

Can our neighbors recognize that we are God's dear children? Are they careful of the jokes they tell in our presence? Does our observance of God's day, week after week and year after year, act as a knife cutting into them? Are we, in fact, walking as lights in the world and showing up darkness in all its ugliness?

WIVES, SUBMIT . . . HUSBANDS, SUBMIT
Ephesians 5:17–33

The main thrust of this section is found in the command: 'Be filled with the Spirit!' (5:18). In explanation, Paul appends several ways in which this filling with the Spirit is to be manifested: 'speaking . . . singing . . . giving thanks . . .

submitting' (5:19–21). In verse 22 he begins to amplify the matter of submitting, wives being first mentioned. But let us not forget that the apostle is here describing what it means to be 'filled with the Spirit.'

What about the submission wives owe to their husbands? Just as surely as God made men and women the same for communion and union, and the same essentially in His eyes through Christ, just as surely in His economy He made them to have different functions. The husband is to lead, in love, even in the matter of Christian growth. The wife is to follow, to submit to him in reverence. A marriage is not complete in God unless both of these aspects are present. If a woman is bristling under the command of God to submit, perhaps the man is not leading her, teaching her and loving her as his own body, or as Christ leads and teaches and loves the church.

However, husbands should refer back to verse 21! In a sense, they should as Christians be submissive to their Christian wives in a horizontal relationship under God! In this sense every Christian is to be submissive to every other Christian, seeking in humility to regard others as better than himself.

And the first duty of husband and wife alike is submission to God! They are the *wife*, remember, and He is their *Husband*.

How is it with us? Maybe we should be asking whether we really know what it means to be 'filled with the Spirit.'

CHILDREN, OBEY . . . PARENTS, TRAIN
Ephesians 6:1–9

Paul is still talking basically about the way in which we are to give evidence that we are filled with the Spirit, amplifying even more this factor of submitting to one another.

Children are to submit to their parents. But even as Paul says this he finds that he has to insert instructions to parents to bring up their children in the nurture of the Lord. They are to feed them on the Bread of Life, and to bring them up in the admonition and warning concerning the Lord and His judgment.

The teaching of submission is carried on through to the servant-master relationship. It is a teaching everywhere present in God's Word. God has set up some to be leaders and some to be followers. He has made some to command and some to obey. As the child learns in the home to submit and obey, he will be prepared to perform this role as student, as employee and as citizen. It may be that some day, according to the gifts given to him, he himself will fulfil the role of teacher, or employer or ruler, or of parent! Learning to submit to those whom God has placed over him is important now and also as preparation for a possible future role.

Indeed, it is a counterpart to his fulfilling the role of obedient child of God! To use the reasoning of John the Apostle, how can we obey God whom we cannot see, if we do not obey our parents whom we can see?

Being an obedient child will not come easily, even in a Christian home. Obedience needs to be taught around-the-clock, and the best teacher will be the parent who himself has learned what it means to be obedient to the heavenly Father.

ONE IN SPIRIT AND PURPOSE
Philippians 2:1–16

A woman who married in her late thirties was questioned about the change that marriage had brought to her life. She revealed that marriage had made her realize how very self-centered her life had been before. Now every thought was turned outward to the needs of her husband and his two children. There was little time for the former concern for self. This was an abrupt experience of change for her. She retained her own interests, but now the emphasis was upon others, not self.

This woman was not complaining, let us hasten to add! She found great joy in her new role and commented upon the understanding and tenderness of her husband in helping her to become the mother of his two teenagers overnight. What was behind her comments was rather a sort of shame at the self-centeredness of her life before her marriage. And she is not alone in this experience.

Some married people never get to the point to which she had come. They remain selfish. They are rigid and defensive. They are not flexible enough to do things just to please their mate, not sensitive enough to perceive his or her emotional and spiritual needs.

Paul gives the Philippians the example of Jesus, who left the courts of heaven for the paths of earth. The Creator faced death for the sake of those whom He had created, those who did not even acknowledge His creatorship! He is the One we should emulate in our marriage, not spending time and effort in weighing each other's actions and motives, but in love giving of ourselves freely, with honest humility.

This is the unity of marriage. This is being 'one in spirit and purpose' (2:2 NIV).

TRANSCENDING MEDITATION
Philippians 4:1–9

Like so much of evil, transcendental meditation has come into prominence at a time when some aspects of its nature or program appear to meet a need. In our world of confusion, mechanization and externals there *is* a need for individuals to learn how to be quiet and think. William Henry Davies in his poem, 'Leisure,' expresses it this way:

> What is this life if, full of care,
> We have no time to stand and stare?

For the Christian, meditation has a quality not known to unbelievers. It transcends all that unbelievers may experience. The meditation of the Christian brings him into communion with God Himself. It is a step away from prayer and often moves into it.

Meditation and prayer are both activities of our minds as well as of our emotions. Paul tells us (4:6) that we are to pour out our pleas and our requests to God. And thanksgiving is to accompany our requests. As we freely turn our minds to God and communicate with Him He will flood our hearts with peace and keep our 'hearts and minds through Christ Jesus' (4:7).

Every part of our thought life is to be characteristically Christian. After all, we are not to be conformed to this world, but rather transformed by the renewing of our minds (Romans 12:2). Paul describes for us what should be the content of our thought: 'Whatsoever things are true, whatsoever things are honest, whatsoever things are just, whatsoever things are pure, whatsoever things are lovely, whatsoever things are of good report: if there be any virtue, and if there be any praise, think on these things' (4:8).

Do our children know that verse? Are they learning to make it a touchstone of their thinking? What about us? Do we meditate in God's law 'day and night'? (Psalm 1:2). The Puritans recognized the value of meditation and it doubtless contributed to their virile Christianity. God's people today need to revive the art.

IN WHATSOEVER STATE
Philippians 4:9–23

How many times we hear of wives who 'just do not like it' where their husband's job requires them to live! We know of enough such wives to call attention to this passage which Paul wrote from prison. 'I have learned,' he says in verse 11, 'in whatsoever state I am, therewith to be content.'

Paul used the word 'state' with reference to situations in which he experienced hunger, thirst, poverty, wealth. He had learned the lesson of adaptability. He was mature. His contentment follows hard on the type of life he has described earlier in the chapter. As he communed with his God, peace flooded his soul, even in a Roman prison.

Is it fitting for a Christian wife, even a minister's wife, to complain about having to live in a certain city or area in which her husband's position has placed them? As helpers to our spouse we need to approach such a situation positively, and build a beautiful home life wherever we live geographically, being mindful that we, like Paul, can *learn* to be content 'in whatsoever state' our Sovereign God has placed us.

To go a step further, we should accept our present living situation as one specifically planned for us by God. He has something for us to learn there. He has someone whose life we may touch with the gospel. Our being in this place was no mistake on His part.

O God, make us content with the place You have chosen for us. Help us to remember that You are there. *This* should be contentment for us.

AS A MOTHER . . . AS A FATHER
1 Thessalonians 2:1–12

Paul says that he and his colleagues had cared for the Thessalonians as gently as 'a nursing mother tenderly cares for her own children' (2:7 NASB). God has placed in the mother-heart a tender concern for her young, even a fierce protective concern that is specially evident in times when danger threatens. In the last day, we are told, there is to be expected a lack of natural affection. When we read of desertion, child-beating, abortion, we know that we are in the last days. Even among mothers who are horrified at these deeds, however, there may be a self-interest that belies the plan of God for the care of little children. Is the mother who seeks employment outside the home *unnecessarily*, leaving her children to baby-sitters, tenderly caring for them?

'. . . You know how we were exhorting and encouraging and imploring each one of you as a father would his own children' (2:11 NASB). Paul goes on to describe further how he and his colleagues dealt with the Thessalonians. Christian fathers are so to deal with their own children. We are reminded of the words of Psalm 103:13,14 in this connection: 'Like as a father pitieth his children, so the Lord pitieth them that fear him. For he knoweth our frame; he remembereth that we are dust.' Fathers are to remember that their children, like themselves, are dust and that they are born in sin. Fathers are to take the frailties of their children into account, showing patience along with firmness, and being ever so careful not to require more than the child can be expected to give!

Mother, how much do you care for your little children, for their souls as well as their bodies? Fathers, do you really try to put yourselves in the place of your children? How much encouragement do you give them? Do you urge them to live lives worthy of God? Or do you leave these tender functions to your wives? What is the depth and quality of your concern for your children?

WOMAN'S PLACE
1 Timothy 2

Here Paul is giving Timothy something of the same advice he gave the Corinthians with reference to the appropriate behavior of women. What do we say about these apparently chauvinistic comments?

First, we say that a consistent view of the divine

inspiration of Scripture rules out our considering these viewpoints as coming solely from Paul. They come from God Himself. If we have complaints, they must be made against the divine Author.

We are, then, faced with the task of understanding just what God is saying to us here, so that we do not dishonor Him in our lack of perception of His character. What is said about the position of women is very clear. But do we understand the reasoning in verses 13 to 15?

First of all, Paul reminds us that the man was made first. Eve was actually taken out of him and made to be his helper. Woman's position is rooted in creation itself.

Second, the circumstances of the entrance of sin instruct us in the position of women. Eve, designed to be a follower, became leader. She was the one who had direct contact with Satan and who was deceived by him. And even as she capitulated to Satan she led Adam in the way of sin.

William Hendriksen in his Commentary on this chapter succinctly analyzes the position of woman today in the light of the fall: 'And now that which before was an unmixed blessing—namely, that Eve, by virtue of her creation, constantly followed Adam—is an unmixed blessing no longer; for now she who, by her sinful example, chose *to rule* him who at that moment was still her *sinless* husband, *must obey* the creature of her own designing, namely, her *sinful* husband.'

But what does verse 15 mean? Hendriksen explains this curious phrase 'saved in child-bearing' in a way which ties in with the context beautifully. He points out that in the bearing and nurture of children the woman finds her greatest happiness. Here, not in the church, she exerts her influence. The woman as a daughter of Eve (whose name means 'the mother of all living') has been equipped by God physically and spiritually to be a mother. As she trusts in God's covenant promise she finds joy in bringing forth children and rearing them in His truth. In the role of homemaker, helper, mother, she exercises her faith and works out her salvation.

This is her sphere! The sphere of the man includes leadership in the church and state as well as the home. But the sphere of the woman is, in general, the home. This concept accords with the picture of the ideal woman of God that greets us in this chapter as well as elsewhere in Scripture: one who is modest and unobtrusive, submissive, one whose good works are the quiet performance of loving deeds, for the immediate family first of all and for the larger family as the need arises.

O God, help women today to give You thanks for their role! Help them to be beautiful in their submission and in their mothering, as You planned for them to be.

ELDERS AND DEACONS AND THEIR HOMES
1 Timothy 3:1–13

Paul is giving young Timothy, his protégé, instructions for the choosing and training of elders and deacons. These requirements, however, are to be considered the norm for all Christians. They are set forth here for church leaders because of the example these men set in the Christian community. But there is no double standard. God holds all Christian men responsible for living according to the patterns here described!

Probably the most significant verses for our purposes are verses 4 and 12. Elders and deacons are to manage their households well and see that their children obey them! As we look honestly at the families of some of our church leaders, we are ashamed. No wonder our churches are often not managed well, when those who have this responsibility do not manage their own households well!

At this point, however, we must recall what we discovered in the Old Testament. In some instances the children of faithful parents did not follow in their father's ways. And God, the perfect Father, speaks of His own rebellious children!

We must also remember that basically the responsibility of maintaining a proper relationship with God rests with the individual child! No one can place all the blame for his own delinquency on his parents.

Still further back, we must go to the sovereign grace of God in redemption!

But the parents must *try!* This is Paul's point. Fathers must be bold, strong, diligent! They must strive to be consistent teachers and disciplinarians in the home. God is a covenant-keeping God. He has given us means which He blesses according to His own good pleasure in the salvation of souls. Leaders in the church must set the example of prayerful, diligent training in an orderly framework. Theirs is not the task of converting their children. Theirs is the task of managing their households in such a way that their children may be expected to respond to the gospel as it is offered!

Do we pray for the leaders in our churches, and for ourselves as we appoint them, or as we seek to support and emulate them?

DEPENDENTS
1 Timothy 5

What a practical book the Bible is! God provides for the nitty-gritties as well as for the so-called 'spiritual' aspects of the lives of His people.

A man's basic function in the human economy is to work to earn a living for himself and his family. Nowhere in God's revelation are we given the impression that an attitude of vague 'trusting the Lord' for our daily provisions is permissible without first applying ourselves as diligently as the ant to laying up store for self and family. The Book of Proverbs calls a man a fool who is lazy and does not exert himself energetically in his work or handle his financial affairs wisely.

We must not only follow this pattern for ourselves but we must teach it to our children. Parents can be too *soft* in the training of their children! Regular hours, good health habits, the faithful performance of a task, the careful use of money, all enter into preparation for a life of adult responsibility.

Some day, in the providence of God, we may be recipients of help from our children! If it proves necessary, we must not be fiercely proud. This is all part of God's plan for the care of His people. We must then give thanks to Him and to our children who are the agents through whom He is providing for His own. We must give thanks, too, for His grace in having enabled us to give to our children in their youth training which contributed to their sense of responsibility and their ability to help to provide for their needy parents.

God's special provisions for dependents are spelled out as carefully as those of our Internal Revenue Service! But they are so much simpler and more beautiful!

EQUIPMENT FOR THE PARENTAL TASK
2 Timothy 1:1–14

Do you ever shrink back in fear as you rear your children? Do you feel afraid that you will make awful mistakes that will hinder their development into normal persons and stalwart Christians? Sometimes, the more we read about child psychology and education, the more awesome the task of the parent appears to us.

Actually this is a wholesome attitude to have. We ought to be aware of the magnitude of the task and the seriousness of it. Parenthood is not something we breeze into gaily. It is something we embark upon carefully and prayerfully.

However, the Christian faith is a kind of package deal. We cannot take certain things only and then feel satisfied that we have the complete kit. We can read our Bible carefully and see all we need to know as parents about the nature of man, the insidiousness of sin, God's dual instruments of love and discipline and the rest. We can know all the answers to child-rearing, and yet not be good parents.

What we need further is also part of the package. We need the ability to apply these principles! We need a gift from God to take all our knowledge and use it! 2 Timothy 1:7 explains this gift so well that it would be worth our memorizing it: 'God hath not given us a spirit of fear; but of power, and of love, and of a sound mind.'

We do not approach our task as parents weighed down with fear. We approach it equipped with power and love and self-control, given us by God for applying His truth to our task.

Surely this was the equipment of Lois and Eunice! It would appear that Timothy's father was not much involved in the boy's training and that the grandmother and mother faithfully brought up the lad to know and love God. The Lord has given parents today this equipment, too. Let us use this gift.

OLDER MEN AND WOMEN
Titus 2:1–5

Are you an older man? God would have you to 'be temperate, worthy of respect, self-controlled, and sound in faith, in love and in endurance' (2:2 NIV).

Are you among the older women? God would have you to 'be reverent in the way' you 'live, not to be slanderers or addicted to much wine, but to teach what is good.' Then you 'can train the younger women to love their husbands and children, to be self-controlled and pure, to be busy at home, to be kind, and to be subject to their husbands, so that no one will malign the word of God' (2:3,4,5 NIV).

These are precious teachings for us. But the wonderful thing about this chapter is the way verse 14 draws everything together to supply a tremendous motivating purpose to each part. Christ 'gave himself for us to redeem us from all wickedness and to purify for himself a people that are his very own, eager to do what is good' (2:14 NIV). This is why the older men and women are to live exemplary lives! This is why the older women are to teach the younger women to provide homes where tomorrow's Christians may be schooled, Christians whose lives exhibit the purity and eagerness to do good which should characterize Christ's people.

Old age is not a time for self-pampering, for unlimited relaxation. It is not a time exclusively for indulging in the hobby for which busier days allowed little opportunity. It is a time in which the stability and dignity and self-control and temperance developed through the years by the grace of God may shine forth as 'the fruit of the Spirit' before younger people so that their sights may be set, and so that we together may be a people that are Christ's, 'eager to do what is good.'

ASSEMBLING TOGETHER
Hebrews 10:19–29

The author of Hebrews brings to bear upon our consciousness the greatness and the wonder of our access to God through His Son. He tells us that since we have in Christ Jesus such a great high priest we should draw near in faith and not waver.

In this context of worship and access to God we read in verse 24 concerning the social aspect of our worship. We are to 'consider how to stimulate one another to love and good deeds' (NASB). God is concerned that the body of Christ be closely knit and that in its oneness there should be also the development of its variety and diversity as each member is encouraged to develop his own gifts and demonstrate the fruit of the Spirit who dwells within.

Then He reminds us of the need of 'assembling together' so that we may encourage one another (10:25 NASB). The concept of the church as a family is nowhere better brought out. We in the church *are* a family; let us function as a family. We read laments that the home is where we hang our hat, the place where mother and dad greet each other at the door as one comes in and the other goes out. We read of the need for togetherness, family living, communication. If these are needs in the human family so are they needs in the family of God. Should we not provide greater opportunity for assembling informally in circumstances where we can better 'stimulate one another to love and good deeds'?

Have we sons or daughters who *do* forsake the assemblies of God's people? It is our responsibility while they are living in our household to insist that they change their ways! But perhaps we ourselves have a low estimate of the church and its people. We must remember our need of the other members of the family!

THE HARVEST OF DISCIPLINE
Hebrews 12:1–13

We have seen that chastening was a prominent theme in the Old Testament, but neither is it lacking in the New. In fact the author of Hebrews is quoting from Old Testament sources in this very section. God is the same yesterday, today and for ever. He still chastens His children.

Why does God discipline us? 'God disciplines us for our good that we may share in his holiness' (12:10 NIV). We speak of the Bible and prayer and the sacraments as means of grace, and so they are. But when illness and bereavement and financial reverses and disappointment come to us, do we recognize these as means of grace, too? These are instruments of God's discipline by which He teaches our stubborn hearts lessons we should have been able to learn by precept. They are stern but necessary agents in our sanctification.

'This is the will of God, even your sanctification' (1 Thessalonians 4:3). He would have us to be holy, even as He is holy. He tells us this in His Word. He pleads with us. He seeks to stimulate us by His demonstrations of love and faithfulness. But often it is only discipline that will wake us up and drive us to our knees before Him.

So it is we are made to see that His discipline is 'for our good that we may share in his holiness.'

[263]

So it is that we need to chasten our children for their good and that they with us may share in the holiness of God.

GOD'S MIRROR
James 1

James gives us many pictures! We have seen how God used the stones in the river and how He used the rainbow. We know how Jesus used the bread and the wine and the shepherd and the sheep. James uses the sea tossed in the wind—perhaps the sea of Galilee. Later in the book he uses ships and fountains and fire. In this section he uses the mirror.

The mirror he had in mind may have been made of polished metal rather than glass. But even if it was not as good a reflector as our mirrors, it still showed up the dirt smudges and the unkempt hair.

Do our children wonder what good it does to read the Bible? Have them look in the mirror. Then go on to the practical precept of verse 25. Looking in the mirror is not enough to change us. We were acquainted with a scholar who read the Bible in seven languages yet continued in his unbelief. People may attend several Bible studies a week and yet show little growth. The good in reading and studying God's Word lies in obeying the God who speaks in it. As we see the smudges we need to cleanse ourselves from them. We need to comb that disheveled hair.

This is the lesson of James the teacher. 'Faith, if it hath not works, is dead' (2:17). His lesson is for us today and for our children.

ACT AS FREE MEN
1 Peter 2

Peter was writing to Gentile Christians scattered throughout the ancient world, persecuted, aliens in a hostile empire. He wrote to show them how they might *witness*. As he put it, he wrote to show them how they might 'proclaim the excellencies' of God (2:9 NASB) and how they might by their behavior cause men to 'glorify God' (2:12 NASB).

How were they to do this? Verse 13 tells us one way: 'Submit!' They were to submit to the emperor. If servants, they were to submit to their masters. Their testimony was to be found in a mild spirit which would strive to imitate Christ's example. 'While being reviled, he did not revile in return; while suffering, he uttered no threats, but kept entrusting himself to him who judges righteously' (2:23 NASB).

We need to read and re-read the life of Jesus, to counteract our sinful distaste for submission—whether we are children who bristle at the requirements of parents, students who chafe at school rules, wives who resent their husbands' rightful headship, or citizens who flaunt civil regulations. In Christ we see God Himself, crucified on a tree He made, by men He made, to save sinners from the punishment they deserve. He did not come to be served. He came to serve, and 'to give his life a ransom for many' (Matthew 20:28).

To submit is to act as free men, who are bond-slaves of God! Are we free? Or do we shudder at the very sound of the word submission? Let us look long upon Jesus, the suffering servant.

THAT THEY MAY BE WON
1 Peter 2:18—3:2

Only when we have read chapter 2 can we understand chapter 3. Chapter 2 tells men to submit patiently to masters, even though they are 'unreasonable' (2:18 NASB). Here in I Peter 3:1 wives are told to submit to their own husbands, even though those husbands are 'disobedient to the Word' (NASB).

The same reason applies in both instances. Chapter 2 makes it clear that by our behavior men may see our good works and glorify God. Our submission is part of our testimony. In the context of marriage the same thing holds good. By her 'chaste and respectful behavior' (3:2 NASB) even without a volley of verbal testimony, the wife may be the instrument God will use to bring an unbelieving husband to Himself.

How often we see among God's people the sincere, devout Christian woman whose burden it is to have a husband who does not share her faith! Sometimes he allows her to go her way. More often, perhaps because her very presence is a constant reminder to him of his own deep spiritual need, he makes her life difficult by either subtle or blatant acts of spite.

What must this woman do? Surely she will pray for this man. Surely she must maintain her own relationship to God and His people. Surely, when she is able, she must give a gentle, honest verbal testimony. But God will probably use more than anything else the silent testimony of her godly life as a cooperative and submissive helper.

If a wife whose husband does not know her Saviour reads these words, let her read on to verse 12: 'The eyes of the Lord are upon the righteous, and his ears attend to their prayer.' Let her read on further to verses 14 and 15: 'But even if you should suffer for the sake of righteousness, you are blessed. *And do not fear their intimidation. And do not be troubled, but sanctify* Christ as Lord in your hearts, always being ready to make a defense to every one who asks you to give an account for the hope that is in you, yet with gentleness and reverence' (NASB).

SHE IS A WOMAN
1 Peter 3:1–15

Let us not for a moment be taken in with the contemporary views which slough off the God-created differences between men and women!

[267]

The very word *unisex* is not only unrealistic, it is unchristian. Peter says that, since 'she is a woman,' the husband (who is a man) is to live with her 'in an understanding way, as with a weaker vessel' (3:7 NASB).

There will be times when physical distress will overtake the wife. Let the husband be understanding. There will be times when emotional stresses will descend upon her as a deluge! Let the husband learn how to help her.

God has given the husband the responsibility of leadership. He expects him to lead his wife in paths of righteousness, as a good shepherd does. He has given the husband strength. He expects him to protect and shield his wife from neighbors, from family, from troubles that press down upon her. At times she will need to be protected against her own fears and frustrations and tensions. 'She is a woman.' He must be understanding.

The husband is set by God in this position of leadership, just as the woman is set by God to be his cooperative helper. Let not the man in his zeal for leadership expect her to call him 'lord' unless he is ready to 'grant her honor as a fellow-heir of the grace of life'! (3:6,7 NASB)

Inconsistencies in living in accordance with God's economy for the redeemed home will hinder our prayers. Each of us must assume the place God has designed for him if the spiritual life of the home is to flourish.

And note, when woman is called the 'weaker vessel' there is an implication that man is a weak vessel, too! Each of us is completely dependent upon the strength of God. 'When I am weak,' Paul wrote, 'then I am strong' (2 Corinthians 12:10 b).

WALK IN THE LIGHT
1 John 1

John probably did not have marriage in mind when he wrote this chapter. But it may very appropriately be applied to marriage.

Think of a bonfire at night in the midst of a field. Those who are close to the fire can see one another well and enjoy together the light and warmth. Someone who is near the fire cannot see as distinctly another who is at the edge of the field or in the woods beyond. That one cannot rejoice with him in the light and warmth.

'If we walk in the light as he is in the light, we have fellowship one with another, and the blood of Jesus Christ his Son cleanseth us from all sin' (1:7). God is our light. If husband and wife are close to Him their fellowship will be precious indeed. If they are at the fringes of His light, or if they are in the darkness of unbelief, such fellowship is impossible. Nor is this rich fellowship in the Lord possible if only one of the two is a believer.

Where are we in relationship to the Light of the World? Are we walking close to Christ? Light stands for holiness and for knowledge. Do our lives radiate holy living and knowledge of the truth?

What about our relationship with one another? There *is* a correlation, John says. If we are not satisfied with our relationship with one another we had better see first of all whether we both are really walking in the light with God.

BROTHERLY LOVE
1 John 4

John's writings embody some of the most beautiful thoughts in Scripture. He probably speaks more about love than does any other Biblical writer. In fact, 1 John 4 needs to be placed beside 1 Corinthians 13, commonly called the 'Love Chapter', for its in-depth treatment of love.

Yet as this chapter is read souls are probed to the point that Christians, as they apply John's searchlight to themselves, sometimes raise questions concerning their own salvation.

Verse 20 is a good verse to use as an example of what we mean. John applies that ugly word *liar* to someone who says 'I love God' but hates his brother. In the same breath he states categorically that such a person 'cannot love God whom he has not seen' if he 'does not love his brother whom he has seen' (NASB).

What kind of relationship do we have with our brothers and sisters, and with those of our spouse? With our parents and the parents of our spouse?

Would it appear from these relationships that we really love God?

What about our children? Do they really love one another? How deep are their rivalries and jealousies? Do those barbs spring from gentle camaraderie or from deep-seated animosity? Are we teaching them, as some moderns do, that it is normal to hate your parents and brothers and sisters sometimes? Or are we showing them that hatred is sin and that sin is poison in the heart?

'And this commandment we have from Him, that the one who loves God should love his brother also' (4:21 NASB). What about our brothers in the larger family of God?

NO GREATER JOY
3 John

In a national weekly newspaper there was an article called "Joy's Many Faces". Readers had been asked to submit the three things that contributed most to their happiness. Among the things that were named several times were books, nature, art, music, friendship, good health, and accomplishment. Many of the notes were beautiful, humorous, poignant. What if the apostle John had written in? His note would have read: 'I have no greater joy than to know that my children walk in truth'.

John, now elderly, had many children in the faith. Gaius was one of them. Gaius was showing in his life a robust faith. John had heard this from some Christian brothers who had seen Gaius and were happy to report his continuing faithfulness to the truth in doctrine and life.

Here John comes forth with that beautifully warm verse which strikes a responsive chord within every true minister of the gospel: 'I have no greater joy than to hear that my children are walking in the truth' (v.4 NIV).

But those of us who have children according to the flesh thrill to this verse, too! To bear children and struggle with their training through the years . . . to see them make a confession of faith . . . to see them weather periods of doubt and rebellion . . . to see them settling down into maturing faith . . . to know that they are 'walking in the truth'—what greater joy can a parent have?

These children are doubly our children, after all. They are children after the flesh and children after the faith, too.

This joy makes the joy of art, of music, of books, and of all other things beautiful and worthwhile, pale into insignificance!

THE MARRIAGE SUPPER OF THE LAMB
Revelation 21

How could God describe to our sin-darkened minds the New Jerusalem? How could He invoke in us a response to the triumph, the beauty, and the wonder of it all? He chose to describe it as a 'bride adorned for her husband' (21:2).

[272]

One day the dwelling of God will be with men and God Himself will live with His people. They will be His people in a new sense and He will be their God in a way never before known. 'He that overcometh shall inherit all things: and I will be his God, and he shall be my son' (21:7). God the Father speaks here.

What, really, is this Holy City, the New Jerusalem of which we read? 'Come hither. I will show thee the bride, the Lamb's wife.' (21:9). 'And he showed me that great city, the holy Jerusalem descending out of heaven from God' (21:10).

In this Book of Revelation, a book of climax, God continues His metaphors of the family. We, His church, the bride, will celebrate our marriage with the Lamb of God, His only-begotten Son, at the marriage supper! The marriage relationship, existing now in figure, will then be consummated. No more will we need to be reprimanded for spiritual adultery. Forever we will be completely true to our Husband who has always been completely true to us!

THE GARDEN OF TOMORROW
Revelation 22:1–7

There is a resurgence of interest in gardens. Surfeited with technology, prompted by interest in ecology, or driven by economic pressure, we are finding joy in the role of gardener. The labor is wholesome exercise. The thrill of employing our God-given creativity grips us. And how delicious the freshly-picked corn and tomatoes taste!

God's Book began in a garden and it ends in a garden. Sin entered the first garden and the ground was cursed. There will be no curse in the Garden of Tomorrow. All will be healed.

God lit the Garden of Eden by the sun and the moon and the stars. He Himself will be the light in the Garden of Tomorrow.

There will be fruit-trees in the Garden of Tomorrow, just as there were in Eden. Among them will be the Tree of Life. There will be no seraphim to keep sinful men from the Tree of Life. Sinful men will not be in the Garden at all. The tree of Life will be available to all in the Garden, and all who eat will live forever in the presence of God.

We were all in the first garden with Adam, our representative. Since we are all members of the human race we were there, every one of us. But entrance into the Garden of Tomorrow is not automatic or universal. Will we be there to enjoy the light of God? Will we be there to eat, finally, of the Tree of Life?

Will I? Will you? It is His redeemed children who will be there and they shall serve Him (22:3).

COME!
Revelation 22:7–21

The Holy Spirit of God is holding forth to the world the invitation of the gospel—'Come!' The church, the bride, is holding forth to the world the invitation of the gospel—'Come!'

We read in Isaiah 55 about the water God freely gives. In John 7 the Saviour offers drink to the thirsty. Now we read of the waters flowing out from the throne of God and of the Lamb. Are there any who have been reading God's Word with us these months who have not yet drunk of this living water? Any husband? Any wife?

So much unimagined beauty in marriage and the family is opened up when both husband and wife are married to Christ. When we are in His church we are His bride. He makes our home new. A beautiful Christian home is not something we achieve by applying certain rules or by trying very hard to be sweet and kind. First, we ourselves need to be new creatures in Christ. Then, as we apply ourselves to His truth, His Spirit works not only in us as individuals but in our homes.

Oh, let us not think that our earthly homes will ever be perfect! Blessed and satisfying as they may be, they are still merely shadows of our heavenly home. Perfection and completion await the coming of our Saviour. So it is that not only do the Spirit and bride say 'Come!' to those out of the Way. Also, the bride looks forward to the advent of the Bridegroom and the consummation of all things. To Him she says, 'Even so, come, Lord Jesus' (22:20).